The Art Model's Handbook

The Naked Truth about Posing
for Art Classes and Fine Artists

Andrew Cahner

www.artmodelbook.com

ISBN-13: 978-1-442-16969-2
ISBN-10: 1-442-16969-9

Book Cover design and page layout by Rika Y. Everett.

Painting on front cover: "Trois Couleurs Noir." Oil on canvas. © 2004 Antoine de Villiers. All rights reserved. Used with permission.

Drawing on back cover: "Ursula." Water-soluble pencils, used dry, on parchment paper. Two and a half hour pose. © 2003 Ronald Eyre. All rights reserved. Used with permission.

TABLE OF CONTENTS

Introduction

The Need for a Handbook

Most art models have no training. They just wing it. They learn through trial and error. A few cities have a models guild to assist new models, but most areas do not.

A credible handbook would be helpful for new models as well as for the community of art schools and artists who hire them. So, I wrote this book based on my experience as an art model; interviews with artists, models, and art school management; as well as secondary research from books and websites. There is some good information on the Internet, but also a lot of nonsense, and it is very time consuming to separate the wheat from the chaff.

As my interviews progressed, another need surfaced: guidelines for inexperienced faculty and workshop leaders who work with art models. So, I added a chapter for faculty as well as several appendices, including sample policies.

I was introduced to the world of art modeling six years ago when I took a figure drawing class through a community adult education program. I learned a lot conceptually, but was frustrated with my lack of artistic talent. By attending the class, I became familiar with the role of the art model and developed an interest in modeling.

I have modeled for schools, art groups, professional artists, and photographers. It has been a rewarding experience. I am fascinated with how artists create. I enjoy being part of the process and seeing the results.

My goal is to distill my experiences and research into a coherent and useful guidebook. Of course trial and error will still be part of your creative experience, but this book will enable you to approach the task with greater awareness and professionalism.

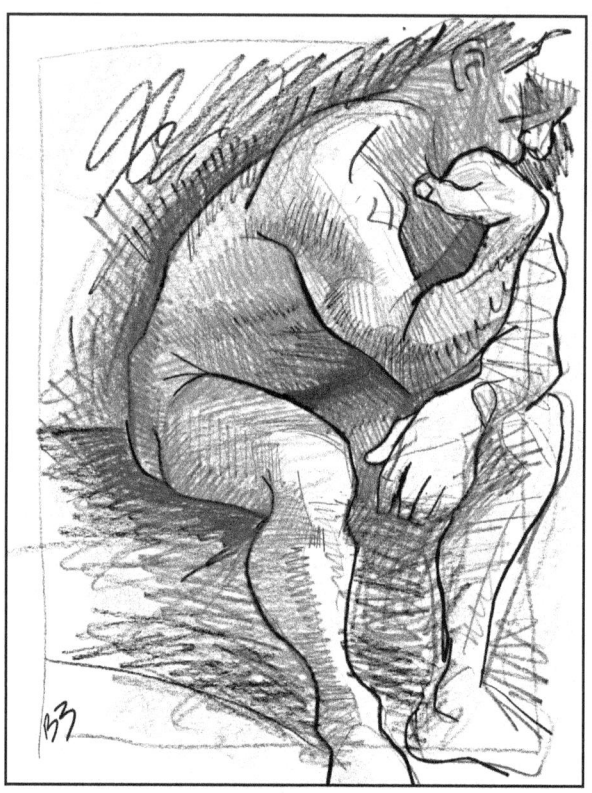

© 2004 Brian Bednarek. Colored pencil sketch.
This pose is based on Rodin's The Thinker.

Chapter 1

Art Models and Figure Drawing

What is figure drawing?

Figure drawing refers to drawing the human body. Life drawing specifically refers to drawing the nude figure. In general usage, the terms figure drawing and life drawing are used interchangeably. Likewise, nude figures are the subject of figure paintings and figure sculpture.

Art classes may use nude or clothed models. Draped and undraped are commonly used synonyms for clothed and nude respectively. Some classes use costume models. In this case, the model provides an interesting wardrobe to pose in.

The majority of figurative art classes hire nude models. Thus nude modeling is the primary focus of this book.

What is an art model?

Art models provide inspiration and visual reference for figurative artists.

Art modeling is not like fashion modeling. Art students need to learn to draw real people, not just the idealized human form. So, just as there are roles for actors of all ages, races, shapes, and sizes, the same is true for art models.

Artists need to develop observation skills in order to draw such a variety of figures. A mantra heard in art classes is, "draw what you see, not what you know." This means that artists should rely on observation rather than memory in order to avoid making every drawing look like the generic human body found in an anatomy book.

All that said, models in good shape may be more in demand because they are likely to have more stamina to hold long or difficult poses. Additionally, lean models with well-defined musculature offer better visual reference for anatomy instruction.

Dancers and yoga practitioners can be great models. Their dance repertoires and yoga postures can inspire graceful, interesting poses. They also tend to be limber and in shape, enabling them to hold the more difficult poses.

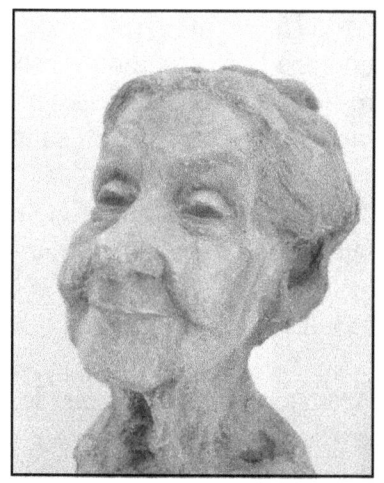

Sculpture of Lalla
© 1995 Auguste Haboush.

Some schools and workshops book only female models. Others are more balanced, alternating males and females. Overall, female models are more in demand than males.

The majority of art models are in their 20s and 30s, but others model well beyond that age. A Los Angeles area model by the name of Lalla Lezli still had bookings at the age of 92, when she died after an automobile accident.

Ronald Eyre has been modeling for artists' groups since retiring as an art teacher. However, at the age of 70, he is scaling back the number of modeling jobs he will accept. "I'm getting a bit stiff in the joints these days. I can't give the full range of poses now that I used to be able to do." He adds, "Despite my age, the Edisbury artists group still assures me that I am an excellent model. This does my confidence a world of good! One has to remember that we as models are not there for artists to view us as perfect physical examples of the human species in its prime, but as fellow human beings, regardless of age. A good model, I feel, would try to portray him or herself *as* a human being with its inheritance of frailty and emotion, and leave artists to make of it as they will. A model can be just as creative as any person with a brush, despite his or her age."

The ranks of art models include Sean Connery, who modeled for the Edinburgh College of Art in Scotland before his movie star career as James Bond.[1.1] However, most art models are not motivated by fame. They tend to play anonymous supporting roles for the artists they serve. The best art models are motivated by the enjoyment of collaborating in a creative environment.

Why do artists draw figures?

I asked some figurative artists to share their views on why the human figure is an interesting subject to draw. Their answers covered a number of themes.

Narrative:

> As an artist I express myself best by drawing or painting and the figure helps tell the story. — Dorothy Wagner

Honesty of the nude:

> I often ask myself that same question. I think because there is nothing more sensitive, powerful, and honest than the nude human figure. — Antoine de Villiers

Aesthetics:

> The human body is a very interesting form. No angle is ever the same. For me, it is the most natural form of architecture. — Aletheia Rio

Expressiveness and emotion:

> Our bodies are so expressive, able to communicate the tiniest nuance of our emotions. — Terry Rafferty

Empathy:

> The human figure is a subject we can all relate to. It speaks a language that all humans understand. — Joseph Larkin

> One of the important qualities of a painter who does figurative work is empathy. The nude can be especially evocative in its removal of all defenses. It allows for a wide range of possibilities, beauty, ugliness, self-consciousness, pride, embarrassment, exhibitionism, freedom of spirit, joy—the entire spectrum of human experience. — John Crowther

Complexity and challenge:

> Human creatures are the most versatile beings on earth, and probably the most difficult to capture onto paper. Therefore, the human figure becomes the most exciting for me to try. — Dee Overly

Others speak of figurative art as the ultimate subject:

> For me, it is the highest form of art. Even when I paint an abstract piece, the shapes, rhythms and contours of the human form are what my brushstrokes follow. — Royce Deans

Anyone who can master drawing the human body well has achieved the highest pinnacle in art, in my opinion.
— Art Krummel

As you can see, figure drawing is about so much more than skin and bones. By understanding the significance of figures in artwork, the model can be a more informed source of inspiration to the artist.

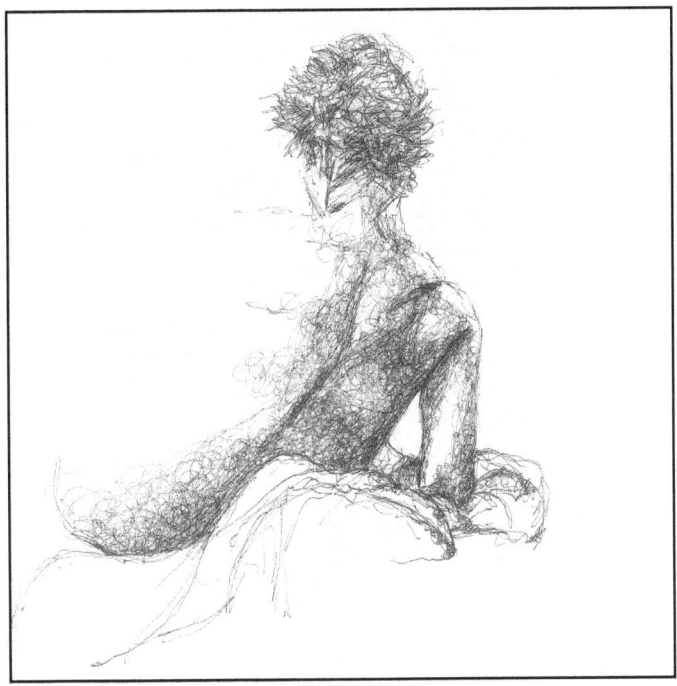

© 2008 Dee Overly. Ink pen sketch. 20 minutes.

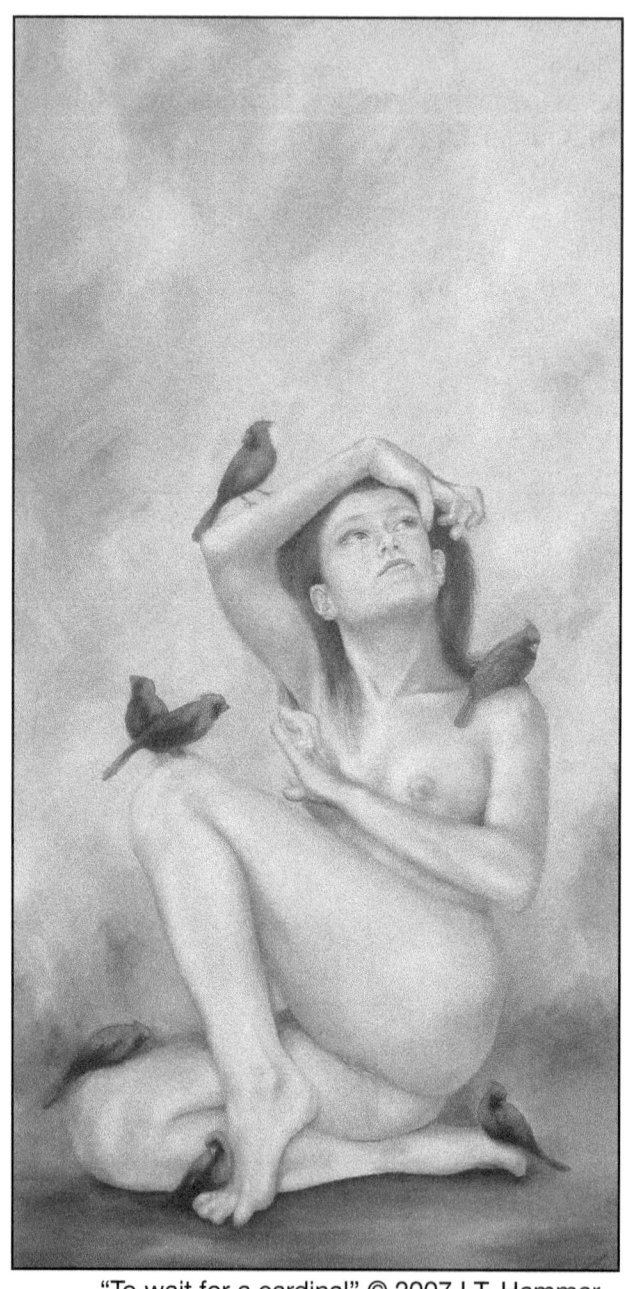

"To wait for a cardinal" © 2007 I.T. Hammar.
Oil on gallery wrapped canvas.

Chapter 2

Nudity and Body Issues

Why do art students draw naked people?

The human form is arguably the most difficult subject for an artist to render. A landscape drawn a little inaccurately will still look like a landscape, but an error in depicting a human likeness will not look right. Capturing an emotional quality is even more challenging. By mastering their figure drawing skills, artists are prepared to draw pretty much anything.

But why draw nude bodies rather than clothed? To learn to draw the human body, one must learn anatomy. One must see how the parts interconnect. One must observe how the body counter-balances when bending.

In addition to the surface anatomy, students also study the skeleton and musculature. Understanding how the bones and muscles fit together greatly improves the artist's ability to observe and draw the subtle bumps, curves, and angles of the human body. Likewise, an artist will be better able to draw a clothed person when he has mastered drawing the underlying body. By studying these things some artists hope to achieve their ultimate goal of drawing the figure without reference. Many masterpiece paintings contain figures drawn without models.

At ease posing nude

"Stage fright is the intense, nearly debilitating fear of appearing ridiculous," according to John R. Marshall, M.D.[2.1] This can be exhibited through a variety of physiological changes, such as accelerated heartbeat and adrenalin rush.[2.2] You need to get over that if you want to be an art model.

The best way to conquer stage fright is to be prepared. There should be no cause for performance anxiety if you understand what the artists are expecting, and you are confident that you can meet those expectations. By reading this book and practicing poses at home, you will solve both problems.

Another social phobia is the human gaze.[2.3] To overcome the fear of being stared at, it helps to consider the artists' perspective. They will be looking at your body parts very intently, but they are not gawking. They are carefully observing their subject. They are identifying shapes and negative spaces, comparing relative values of shadow, and measuring proportions. If you've ever attempted to draw a human likeness, you have an idea how challenging it is.

As mentioned in the previous chapter, the phrase, "Draw what you see, not what you know" is often heard in art classes. You might hear an instructor say this if a student is spending more time looking at her drawing than at the model. Observation is a critical drawing skill. Even though an artist knows you have five toes on your foot, she has to look carefully to see that only three are visible from her vantage point.

You need to be at ease and nonchalant about nudity. If the thought of posing nude in a roomful of artists makes you nervous or fearful, it would be wise to deal with this anxiety before accepting a figure modeling assignment.

Spending some time at a nude beach, hot spring, or nudist resort might help you get used to being nude around other people. The Naturist Society promotes a culture of body acceptance and the belief that the nude human form is inherently wholesome and natural. You may find its website helpful in coming to terms with your own body acceptance issues: www.naturistsociety.com.[2.4]

I don't mean to imply that all art models are nudists—most probably wouldn't identify themselves as such. Furthermore, while nudists are at ease with their bodies, that is not the only qualification for being a good art model. Art modeling is first and foremost about holding interesting poses.

Be sure that you are committed before accepting a gig. Don't chicken out and cancel at the last minute, or freak out on the dais. The instructor and the students are relying on the model to be dependable.

Erections

Men who are curious about art modeling have asked what would happen if they got an erection while posing nude. A classroom is not a sexual environment. An erection would be inappropriate.

Here's what the United Kingdom-based Register of Artists' Models (RAM) Consultative Guidelines say about the topic:

> RAM members are nearly always suspended from the Register following a complaint about this. We are aware that there are a number of male models who genuinely believe that there is no acceptable reason to find erections offensive, but we find that the opinion of tutors, students and artists is overwhelmingly against them, and our policy reflects this.[2.5]

My advice is not to obsess about it. Models are humans, not mannequins. Male genitalia may retract during dynamic poses and expand a little bit during a relaxed pose under a warm spotlight. This is taken in stride. Don't make an issue of it.

The acceptance of an erection in a private art group may vary. In her article How to Become an Artist's Model, artist Kelly

Borsheim writes, "I have never been in a session in which that happened that anyone commented aloud on it."[2.6]

An erotic drawing group is one setting in which an erect model may actually be requested. While this genre is outside the scope of my experience, I am aware that such groups exist.

Menstruation

Women must consider their comfort with modeling nude during their periods. Kelly Borsheim addresses the topic:

> Menstruation: to model or not to model? That is the question. And that is up to each individual model. Some models have told me they just use a tampon and insert the string so no one is the wiser. Another model told me that a certain date (to work) was out of the question because her period was expected and for her, that meant three solid days of excruciating pain at home. From the artist's point of view, the worst thing you can do if you want to keep working is to not show up. If you choose not to work during this time of the month, then *please* do not schedule a session then. Just say you are not available. We do not need to know the reason.[2.7]

My perspective on artistic nudes

Nude figures have been the subject of art throughout history.

The nude figure is a timeless image, without fashion clues to define the setting in a given time period. With no uniform to define the social class or employment role, nudity also signifies honesty and authenticity—the naked truth—and one's true self without any façade. Nude figures in nature can represent mankind living in harmony with the environment.

Some people associate nudity exclusively with a sexual context. This is one reason why people are embarrassed about nudity in art. I don't share this mindset. Fine art nudes can be sensual without being erotic. The nude form can also embody a child-like innocence and freedom.

Consider the wholesomeness of Norman Rockwell skinny dipping scenes. Think of fine art nudes by Michelangelo, Auguste Rodin, and Maxfield Parrish. This is the kind of art that inspires me.

Evidence of American society's uneasiness with nudity can be found in art classrooms. Some beginning students will omit the penis from their drawings, as if it doesn't exist. Ironically, in my opinion, this inaccuracy calls more attention to the part of the drawing they are avoiding. This tension seems to fade away as figure drawing becomes routine. Experienced artists are more likely to draw the whole body with confidence, resulting in much more natural and believable works of art.

In her book Live Nude Girl, Kathleen Rooney writes about the distinction between nude and naked. She uses the word naked when referring to the awkward condition of being without clothes. She writes, "I am half-*naked* in my undies, but I am *nude* without any clothes at all... Actual nakedness? I shy away from. Nudity? No problem."[2.8] I agree with her sentiment. There is dignity in the nude form, but when the emphasis is on what it not being worn, the impression can be indecent. I would add that it is the intent of the image, rather than the nudity, that makes it indecent or not. The intent of the pervasive, scantily-clad images in mainstream media is clear—sex sells. I suspect Rodin's intent was quite different when he sculpted The Thinker.

Chapter 3

The Model Bag: What to Bring

There are two mandatory things you should bring with you:

- **Timer** – Models are usually expected to time their own poses. I prefer a digital timer with a numeric keypad, which makes it easy to type in the duration of the pose. Radio Shack sells a 10-Key Count Up/Count Down Timer for under $10.
- **A robe or other cover up** – This is discussed further in Chapter 5, Professional Conduct.

Other items to consider:

- **Sandals** – I recommend wearing sandals to modeling gigs, or to bring a pair in your model bag. Sandals can be put on quickly during a break, and removed quickly when you resume posing. The floors in art studios and classrooms are almost always filthy with charcoal dust, pencil shavings, etc. The soles of your feet will get black if you walk barefoot. Also, students frequently sharpen their drawing materials; you wouldn't want to step on a utility-knife blade in bare feet.
- **Sheet** – to drape over the model stand. This is more for hygiene than aesthetics. A solid color is best, so as not to distract from the pose.
- **Towel** – you might get sweaty sitting under spotlights. You might also drape the towel over a chair before sitting, for the same hygienic reason you drape the sheet over the model stand.
- **Pole** – a common prop for male models, but can be used by females as well. It should be strong enough to support

your weight when you lean on it. Home Depot sells a variety of wooden dowels. A more portable alternative is a paint roller pole, which comes in sections that screw together.

- **Props** – clothesline rope is a handy prop. Tie it to the model stand, and pull on it for poses with great muscle tension. See Chapter 7, Gestures, for more prop ideas.
- **Masking tape** – to mark a pose that will be continued after a break. Sometimes the classroom will have tape, but don't count on it.
- **Water** – Modeling can be a workout, so I bring a refillable water bottle.
- **Snack** – for a long session, you might wish to bring a light snack, such as a banana.
- **Appointment Calendar (and pen!)** – in case you are offered more bookings, you can check to see if you are available and record your new sessions.
- **Exercise mat or yoga mat** – to place on the model stand to make posing more comfortable. For example, kneeling on a wooden platform can be painful after a few minutes. A cushioned mat makes it bearable.
- **Pillow or cushion** – sometimes these are provided in the classroom or studio, but not always. A pillow not only aids in the comfort of a pose, but can also be used to give a slight incline to a reclining pose.
- **Swimwear or underwear** – may be required when posing for minors. Skin-colored fabric is ideal, as light and shadow will blend more subtly with the rest of the body, but color selection is limited for men's garments.

Obviously, if you ride a bicycle or the subway to your modeling gigs, you'll want to pack light.

Chapter 4

The Classroom and Class Structure

The classroom may be set up for drawing, painting, or sculpture. Or as a sign of the times, the room may be set up with computer stations for the students to draw on digital tablets.

The model stand is where you will set up. Sometimes it is against a wall, with easels or benches in a semi-circle around you. Other times, the model stand is in the center of the room with the artists completely surrounding you.

Occasionally two models will pose in the same class on separate model stands. The models could be of the same or the opposite gender. Half of the students will draw one model, and half the other. The instructor may have the models switch stands half way through the class so all of the students can draw each model. There are classes in which two models will share the same stand, but this is not common.

At some venues—but not all—there is a space heater for the model's use. As you can imagine, if the room temperature is set for the comfort of clothed occupants, the nude model may feel colder than the students. Personally, I do not always use the heater. Sessions with lots of dynamic gesture poses can be quite a workout, raising body temperature. If a spotlight is used, that can provide some heat as well. But most models feel more comfortable with a heater most of the time. Whereas some schools and private workshops do not provide them, a well-prepared model may consider investing in a small portable heater to have if the need arises.

Some classrooms are first class, while others are quirky. Some are very well equipped and others are bare bones.

The most unusual classroom in my experience was at Whittier College. The art department was in an old gymnasium building. The gym floor was divided into several studio areas. The figure drawing class was held in the loft, at the top of the bleachers and around the corner. There was no door, and you could look down to the gym floor. It was paradoxically wide open, and yet secluded and private.

The most impressive place I have modeled is Art Center College of Design. Prior to the class, a small army of work-study students arrives to set up the room to the instructor's requirements. This may include setting up a model stand against the wall and hanging a backdrop behind it. Or they may set up the model stand in the middle of the room. They will also deliver any props that had been ordered from their extensive inventory. A heater, a mat, a cushion, and a spotlight are standard equipment. This college has 75 to 100 model bookings per week, and they are very well organized.

Class structure

The model should be on the model stand, all set up and ready to pose, at the start time of the class.

Consult with the instructor before the class to ask if there are any special directives. Each week might introduce a different part of the anatomy. For example, if the class is studying legs, the instructor may ask for standing poses.

Models are usually expected to choose their own poses. While instructors may give some direction, their job is to teach, not to micromanage the model.

The instructor will specify the duration of the poses. A class may start with 10 one-minute poses. It will be your responsibility to assume the poses and time them. Gestures up to two minutes are easier to time by counting the seconds silently. "One one-thousand, Two one-thousand, Three one-thousand." Use your timer for longer poses.

When you are asked to do a set of short poses, go from one pose to the next without pausing. But don't be so rushed that you forget to start your timer.

It is common for a drawing class to begin with very short gesture poses, followed by progressively longer poses. However, some classes do not have any gesture poses. The shortest pose in some drawing classes is five minutes. In painting or sculpture classes, there could be one pose for the entire session, or the same pose for multiple sessions.

A model is not usually expected to hold a pose for more than 25 minutes at a time. After a five-minute break, the model may be asked to resume the pose or start a different pose.

Breaks are a good opportunity to stretch or use the restroom. During a longer break it is fun to walk around the room and see the artwork. Be respectful of each student's stage of development. You are not the instructor, so it is not your role to criticize. Conversely, you must have thick skin if someone draws you too accurately, calling attention to your flaws.

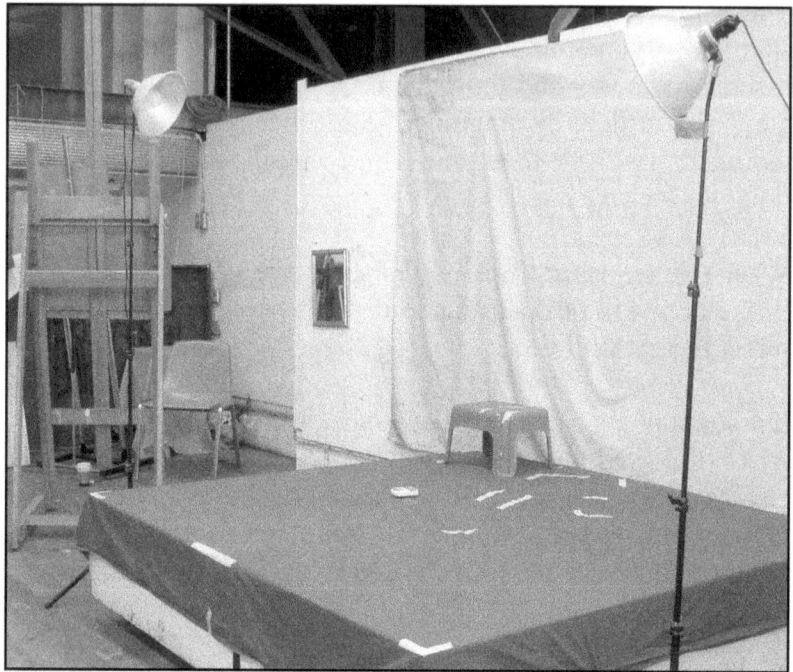

Model Stand. The pose has been marked with masking tape to assist the model in resuming the pose accurately after a break. Masking tape has also been used to mark the corners of the model stand, so the sheet can be aligned properly when the pose is continued on a subsequent day.

Chapter 5

Professional Conduct

Reliability

The model should be on the model stand, ready to model at the start time of the class. If you need 10 minutes to change clothes and get set up, arrive at least 10 minutes before the appointed time.

When a model cancels at the last minute, it creates extra work for the instructor or coordinator to find a replacement. If the model doesn't show up on time—or at all—class time is wasted. In some cases when this happens, students will take turns modeling (clothed). They are paying tuition to attend the class, not being paid to model for it, so the model who doesn't show up is cheating the students in a very real sense.

Maintain an appointment calendar, and honor all commitments by showing up on time and prepared. This is a basic tenet of professionalism in any field, but especially important when a roomful of people are depending on you. If you are not reliable and punctual, you will not get repeat bookings.

The model should expect this diligence and professionalism to be reciprocated, but it doesn't always work out that way. One time I arrived for a class and was surprised to see another model setting up. The model coordinator had double-booked and my name was not on the schedule. I have heard many stories from models with similar experiences, having shown up for bookings only to find out that a workshop was canceled or the model was double-booked.

To avoid this problem, Los Angeles-based model Toni

Czechorosky recommends confirming bookings a few days before. "I always call and e-mail all bookings for the week these days. Better safe than sorry, and it shows you are on top of things."

Cover up

The model should bring a robe or other appropriate cover up. Choose something simple to put on and take off. In a three-hour class with short breaks every 30 minutes, you might get dressed and undressed seven times. Don't make a big production of it.

When posing, the model is nude. Before the first pose and during breaks, the model is covered. While the model might be comfortable wandering around the room nude, that could make the other people in the room uneasy.

The model should not change from street clothes to the robe on the model stand. Some schools provide dressing rooms, or a screened corner of the studio. In other schools, the models change in the restroom.

Professional atmosphere

The model should expect to be treated with respect by the artists or students, and vice versa. Avoid physical contact with students, and refrain from sexually explicit or offensive language. In short, maintain a professional atmosphere.

Touching, pointing, and personal space

Normally the model is provided a few feet of personal space, but there are times when it is appropriate for the instructor to point to features of the model's body, or even touch the model with permission.

The instructor may point out where light and shadows fall. He or she may explain anatomical features demonstrated by the pose, such as the tension in certain muscles or the tilt of the pelvis. Some instructors use a laser pointer. Standard etiquette is that an instructor will not touch a model's body without permission, and students never touch the model.

Some poses last hours, and must be resumed identically after a break. This is common in painting and sculpture classes, but also occurs in drawing classes. It is customary to mark the pose with masking tape or chalk to make it easier to resume exactly the same position. An instructor may offer to tape the pose if the model is unable to do so without breaking the pose.

Don't move

Artists are not just observing your body, they are observing how light and shadows fall on your body. When you move, the light and shadows may shift. From their perspective, it is as if they are drawing an entirely different subject.

Distractions

Drawing requires concentration. The model should not talk while posing. That is not to say that the room should be like a morgue. Often there is background music while the artists are drawing. The instructor might also walk around the room advising students on their drawings. Obviously, the model should respond if the instructor asks a question. But in general, the model should be quiet.

Another form of distraction is eye contact. "Don't move your eyes around," advises Minneapolis-based artist Matt Semke. "Pick a spot on the wall or something and stay focused on it. I hate it when I'm drawing the model's face and all of a sudden there's a weird eye contact moment and the model doesn't seem comfortable. Also, it just helps with keeping your head in the exact same spot."

Stay awake

"My big pet peeve is sleepy models, which happens quite a lot actually," adds Semke. Modeling is a physical exercise and a creative exercise. Both elements require energy, so arrive well rested.

Student work

Students generally need to save their drawings. Their final grade is based on either showing improvement or their best work during the term. Therefore, it is not appropriate to ask students if you can have a drawing.

Cameras

Photography is generally prohibited in figure drawing classes. With private art groups or an individual artist, photographing the pose should only be done with the model's permission. With poses that span more than one day, such as with sculpture, a photo could be used to help resume the pose identically. Other times, an artist may wish to have a reference photo to work from when the model is not present.

Privacy

Care is generally taken to keep gawkers away. The door to the classroom remains shut during the class and window shades are drawn to avoid curious peeks from the hallway. The only time I experienced visitors in the room while I was posing was when another teacher brought in her students to observe the class for around 15 minutes. These were students from a prerequisite class who would be taking figure drawing in the future. The figure drawing instructor gave them a mini lecture and did a demonstration drawing for them. The model should have a professional attitude, and should not be bothered by anyone who has a legitimate reason to be in the room.

If you feel there are inappropriate visitors in the room, if you have security concerns, or if there are any other problems with professional conduct, speak with the instructor or workshop leader to resolve the issue.

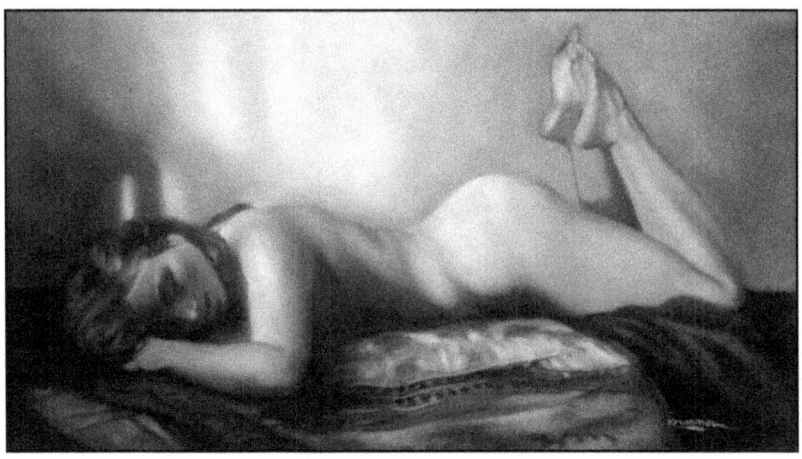

"Miss M" © 2007 Art Krummel. Oil on canvas.

Chapter 6

How to Pose

Duration of pose

It is helpful to divide your repertoire into three categories by duration:

- Gestures – up to three minutes
- Short poses – five or 10 minutes
- Long poses – 15 minutes to several hours.

While the exact cut-off between the categories may be debatable, the distinctions are significant.

Gesture poses are generally very dynamic and off balance. This puts strain on the muscles that is sustainable only for a very short time. The most dynamic poses can be unbearable for five minutes.

Long poses must be very well balanced. You might argue that 15 minutes is not that long. There are poses you could hold for 15 minutes that would be quite troublesome for an all-day painting class. That is certainly true, but it is better to err on the side of sustainability. If you are too ambitious in your pose selection, you may find yourself in agony.

Short poses fall somewhere in between. Your options for a ten-minute pose are more limited than the vast selection you could easily hold for one minute, but can be more ambitious than a pose you might select for 25 minutes.

All this is not to say that an artist may not wish to sculpt or paint a dynamic pose. In that case you would simply pose in relatively short increments, and then take a quick break. Or, you could arrange for some kind of support that would enable you to hold the pose for longer periods of time. Sculptor Kelly Borsheim explains:

> I usually allow models for sculpture to pose for five to 10 minutes at a time. However, I sometimes want more animated poses, so it is a trade off. When I am creating a more dynamic pose, after the initial "whole body" pose—so I can capture the gesture—I often have the model just pose one part of the body while resting another. An example is in my bronze sculpture "Against the Dying of the Light." While I made up the pose based on my own emotions, I eventually used three different models for the piece. I hired dancer and model Todd for his "diamond-like quads." Sometimes I would have him sit on a tall stool and stretch out one leg so that I could get the toes pointed in the right way. That would have been impossible for him to do had he been standing and trying to imitate the gesture in the artwork.

> The point is that creating art takes time and it is not always necessary for the model to sustain the entire pose for the entire time. As long as the artist and model communicate, there should be no problem. Of course, this type of "partial sitting" is more difficult when there is more than one artist involved, but still, communication makes this work at times as well.

I had a similar experience when I was modeling for a professional painter. He wanted me to assume a very contorted pose which included holding one arm above my head. Rather than holding my arm up for several hours, he only asked me to do so while he was painting that arm. I could relax my arm while he was painting the rest of the body.

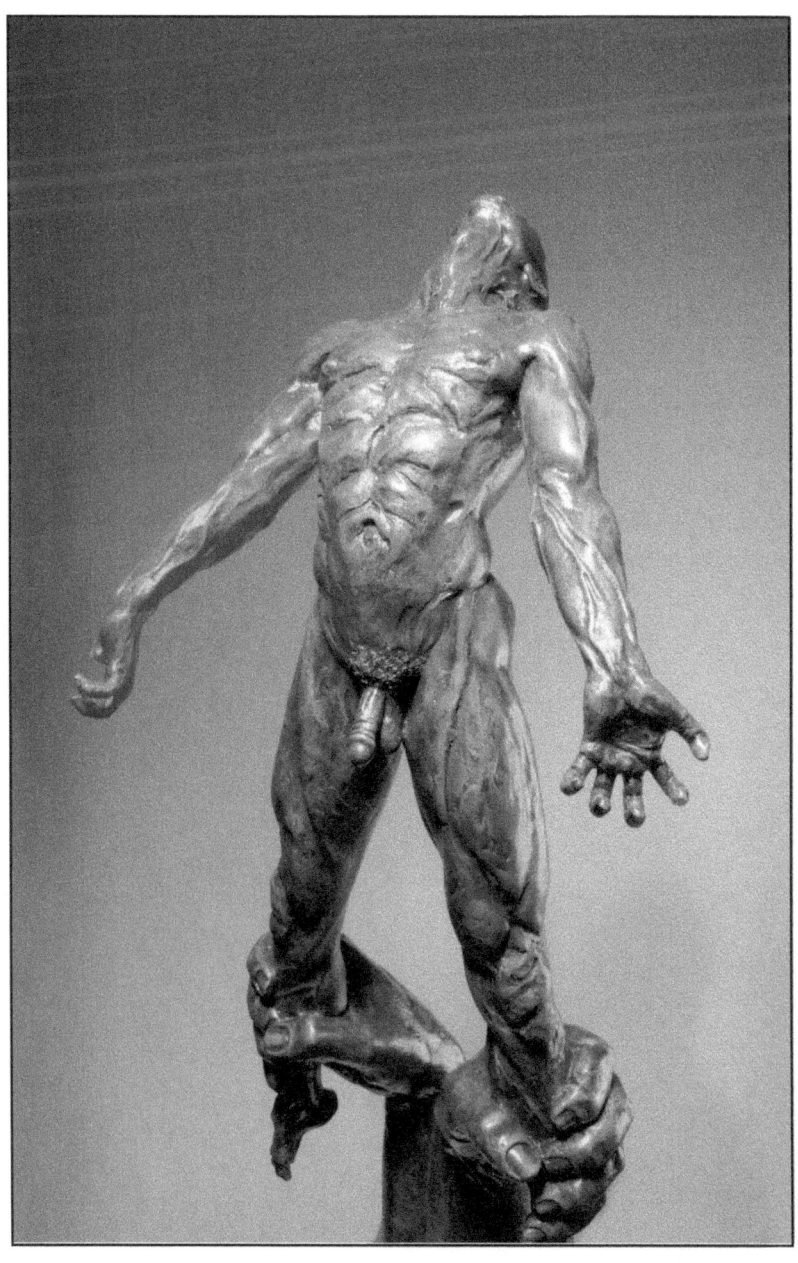

"Against the Dying of the Light" © 2008 Kelly Borsheim.
Bronze with limestone base.

When choosing your own poses for a class, select suitable poses for the required duration. If you are asked to repeat one of your one-minute gestures for a 20-minute pose, be honest about the sustainability of the request. Perhaps you could suggest something similar that is easier to hold. Or perhaps you could suggest a way to add support, such as resting a knee on a chair instead of holding it in mid-air, in order to accomplish the goal.

How to pose

Part of the model's job is to inspire. Sometimes an artist will draw the pose literally, as is usually the goal in a classroom environment. Other times an artist will use the pose as a rough reference and modify or embellish it, add some imagined context, or create some imagined character.

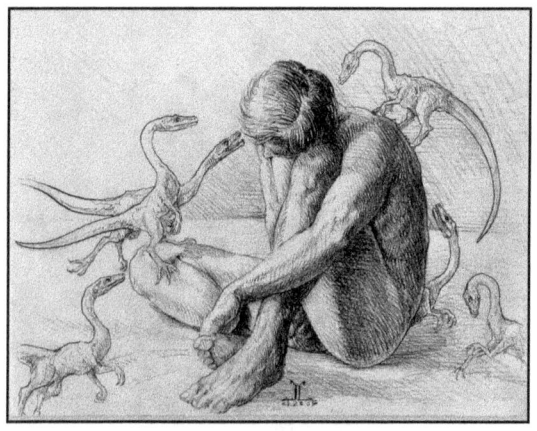

© 2005 Joseph Larkin. Pencil Sketch.

Make sure there are no "cheap seats" in your audience. You don't want artists on one side of the room to draw a boring back pose 10 times in a row. If there are artists sitting 360 degrees around you, rotate your body with each successive pose: for example, face north, then southwest, then east, etc.

Twisting the torso can help to make a pose interesting from multiple angles. Your head, chest, and lower body could be facing three different directions.

The head, hands, and feet are the most difficult things to draw. Keep that in mind when choosing poses. If students are seated behind you, you could move a hand or foot into their view to give them something more interesting to draw.

Vary the height of your poses: standing, sitting, kneeling, reclining.

For very long poses, balanced and sustainable are the operative words. If you are supporting your body weight on one foot or with your arms, or if your arms are raised over your head, the pose will be challenging to hold for an extended period of time. Fortunately, artists often prefer simple, relaxed poses which look natural and genuine, rather than contrived and "posed."

Choose poses that suit your body type. For example, I am not especially muscular so body-builder poses would look silly for me. Some poses are decidedly feminine while others look masculine. Male and female bodies are built differently so some poses are more natural looking and easier to hold for one gender than the other.

Shoot for asymmetry in your poses. This is not to say that poses can never be symmetrical. Crucifixions, for example, have been the subject of paintings for centuries. But in general, asymmetry is a way of adding visual interest.

Common requests

An instructor may request a contrapposto pose. Contrapposto means "counter position" in Italian. Stand with your weight shifted to one leg, causing the pelvis to tilt one side lower than the other. The shoulders will naturally tilt the opposite way to counter-balance. A prime example is Michelangelo's statue of David. See photo on page 103.

Another common request is to include <u>negative space</u> in your pose. Think of the figure as positive space, and any open areas as negative spaces. For example, when you put your hand on your hip with the elbow pointing out, the triangular shape between the arm and the torso is called a negative space. See painting on page 33.

You might be asked to do a <u>foreshortened pose</u> in which part of the body is closer to the artist than the rest. If I pointed my finger at you with my arm fully extended, you would view my hand disproportionately large compared to my shoulder, which is farther away. The entire body can be foreshortened in a reclining pose. If you take a reclining pose in the middle of the room, surrounded by artists on all sides, the artists at your head and feet will see the pose as foreshortened, while the others will not. See drawing below.

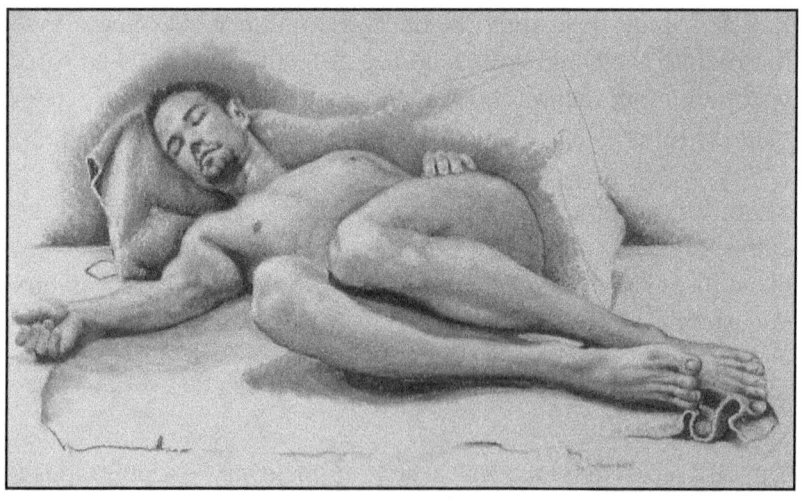

© 2004 Philip Kinzli. Pastel. Foreshortened pose: the feet are closest and appear disproportionately large compared to the head.

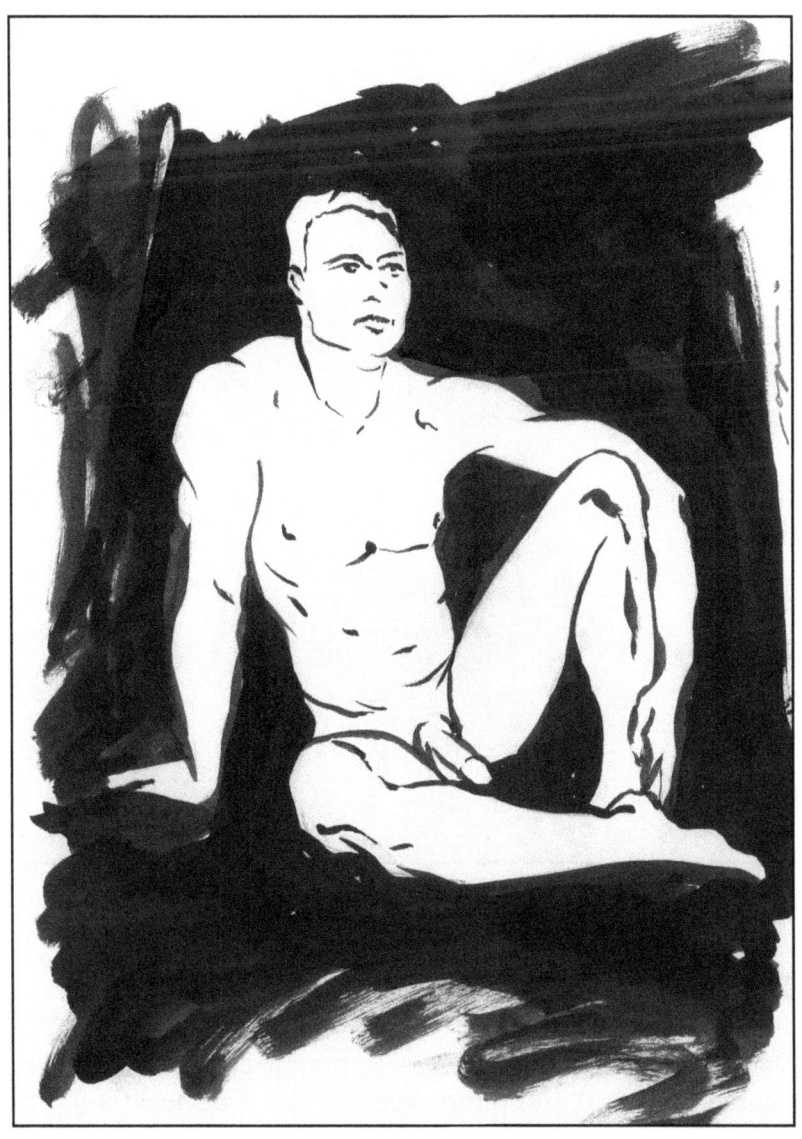

© 2003 Royce Deans. Ink painting.
The black areas are negative spaces.
The figure is positive space.

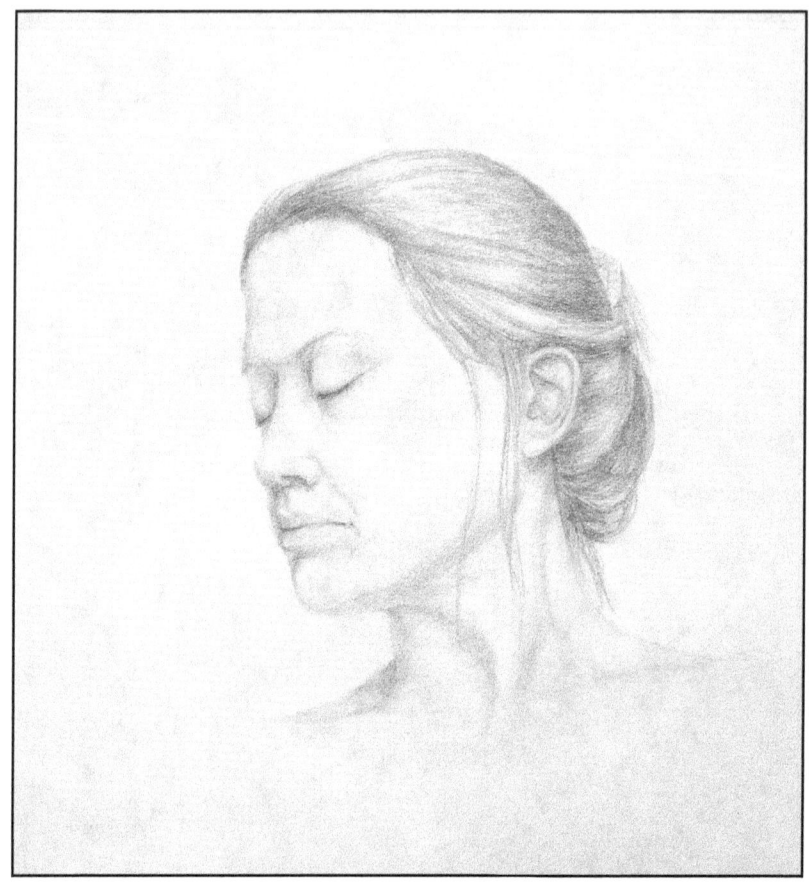

© 2008 Terry Rafferty. Pencil drawing. 20 minutes.

Expression

Body language or facial expression can add emotive qualities to your pose. Poses can express surprise, fear, melancholy, etc.

In a lecture called "A Manifesto," artist Michael Newberry talks about emotion in his art.

> Once I was wracked with three deaths of people close to me. I was emotionally frozen. To change that, I decided

to do a series of drawings based on mourning. The first person I asked to pose for this theme was a model for a class I was teaching. He kind of freaked out when I asked him. And then he told the story that his father had killed his mother and then committed suicide. Imagine doing a drawing based on loss and death with him. How deep I had to go to be truthful. And I had to respect and honor his horrible losses as well as my own.[6.1]

Holding poses

It may sound easy, but it can be physically demanding to sit still and hold a pose. Try holding still for 30 minutes. No really, pick a pose and hold it for 30 minutes. I'll wait.

How did you do? Did you move? Do you regret the pose you selected? Are you feeling sore?

Now you understand the importance of selecting an appropriate pose for the specified duration. Very dynamic, off balance gestures are easy to hold for 30 seconds. A 20-minute pose must be well balanced.

Even the difference between three minutes and five minutes is significant in terms of what pose you can hold. Balance is a critical factor. The more off balance your pose, the more you are exerting your muscles to compensate. It is much easier to hold a well-balanced pose for 20 minutes than to hold a strenuous, dynamic pose for five minutes.

Kathleen Rooney estimates that she held a pose for 111 hours cumulatively for a sculpture class. "Pick a bad pose and you risk ruining your body if you succeed in holding it, or ruining their art if you fail."[6.2]

Know your limits. It's easy to get yourself into a pose that you regret. Once people start drawing, which is usually immediately, it's too late to change your mind. Of course, if you are in severe pain, or simply can't hold the pose any longer, you'll have to break the pose. But if you do this frequently, you won't be a popular model.

The biggest mistake along my learning curve was being too ambitious with unsustainable poses. My intentions were noble, but naïve, and I did have to break poses a couple of times. One time, an instructor ended the pose early out of compassion because he saw my leg muscles quivering. Or maybe it wasn't compassion so much as my suffering was a distraction.

Here are some tips:

- Slight variations in a pose can make it infinitely easier to hold. A slight shift in weight can be the difference between a grueling pose and a comfortable one.

- Don't lock your knees. This can restrict blood flow to the brain causing you to faint.[6.3] Besides, locked knees are not a natural-looking position, so slightly bent knees are better.

- Avoid holding your hands up for an extended period. This is very tiring.

An itch during a long pose can be a nuisance, but your job is to hold still. It is very frustrating to artists if you move your hands when they are drawing them, especially if you don't place them back in exactly the same position.

What are you thinking?

In addition to the physical challenges in holding a long pose, there is a mental aspect. Modeling sessions are typically between three and five hours. If you are modeling for a painting class, you will be still in a single pose for most of that time.

Some people think about all the things they need to do. Some of this book was brainstormed while I was on the model stand. Some people meditate. In a similar vein, I have cleared my head by silently counting down the seconds for 20 minutes. If I lose count, I don't really care, since I'm relying on my timer for an accurate timing.

Whatever you do to pass the time, stay aware of your pose.

Resuming poses after a break

Typically a model is not expected to hold a pose for more than 20 to 25 minutes at a time. However, for painting and sculpture—and for drawing sometimes—the pose must be resumed identically after the break.

Use masking tape to mark the pose. You don't need to use a lot of tape. For example, to indicate the position of your left foot, you could put a piece of tape by your heel and by your big toe rather than outlining the whole foot. Don't just rely on the tape. Remember the pose. Remember the angle of your head and what you were looking at. Make a note of other key landmarks that will help you resume the pose: my right knee is pointing at the guy in the blue shirt; my left foot is facing the door. It is important that you resume the pose with body parts in the same position relative to each other. It is also important that the pose is resumed in the same position on the model stand, so the perspective does not change in relation to where each artist is seated.

Sometimes you are thrown a curveball and are asked to resume a pose as an afterthought. Maybe the artists like the pose and want to develop a more finished drawing. Maybe the instructor wants to correct a drawing as a demonstration. In this case you hadn't marked the pose with tape, so you have to rely on your memory of the benchmarks to resume the pose as closely as possible.

In order to avoid moving your head during a pose, choose something to look at. It could be a light switch, the fifth ceiling tile from the corner, or even your timer. If you have to resume a pose, having a defined object to look at will make it easier to hold your head in the same position.

If you resume a pose differently than you had before the break, the artists may ask you to adjust the pose. They can tell from their works in progress if your pose is inconsistent. But a diligent model will strive to replicate the pose without a lot of micromanagement.

Planning for a continued pose

One time, I was booked by a professional artist who asked me to pose for a life-size oil painting with my arms extended up at a 45-degree angle. Knowing that I would have to resume this pose after a break, I was concerned that my hands needed to be at precisely the same height and angle as the original pose. To facilitate this, I held a pole in each hand, with a piece of masking tape under my thumbs. The pole locations were marked on the floor. This advance planning ensured that an identical pose could be resumed, even on a different day.

My foot is asleep

A body part falling asleep is an occupational hazard for art models. This is a result of putting prolonged pressure on the nerves in that body part. It is analogous to leaving the phone off the hook; eventually the dial tone stops, because the telephone switch recognizes something is amiss with the circuit. This is not usually a serious problem, but prolonged pressure can cause nerve damage.[6.4,6.5]

One little trick I've developed to try to keep hands and feet "awake" is to very subtly wiggle my fingers and toes periodically. You don't want to break the pose by moving the position of your hands or feet, nor do you want to distract the artists.

Another tip: Don't stand up too quickly. If you try to stand when your foot is asleep, you could fall and seriously hurt yourself.

A model should not make a habit of breaking poses. However, if you are in serious pain, and feel that cutting off circulation or pinching a nerve will cause health problems, use common sense. Tell the instructor that you need a break.

Of course, it is even better to avoid the situation in the first place. Poses in which you cross your legs or sit on a foot are asking for trouble.

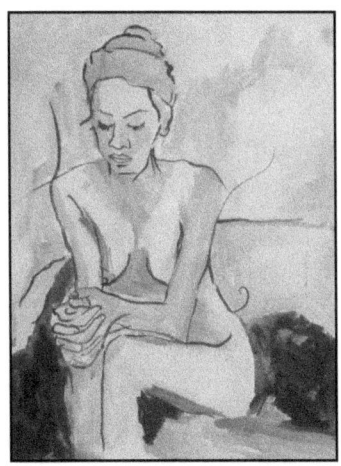

"Jessie" © 2008 Matt Semke.
Watercolor on paper.

Chapter 7

Gestures

Gestures are short poses, often done at the beginning of figure drawing sessions to help the artists warm up and loosen up. Gestures can be as short as 15 seconds or as long as three minutes. One or two minute poses are common.

Gesture poses should be dynamic. The most interesting gestures are asymmetrical, imply motion, and often include extended arms. The shorter the pose, the more ambitious and strenuous the poses can be. It may sound easy to hold a pose for a few minutes, but when the body is off balance, it puts great strain on the muscles. So, even with relatively short poses, it is important to know your body's limits to avoid unnecessary distress or the need to break a pose.

Models with a dance background can use dance steps as inspiration. Graceful ballet movements would make excellent gesture poses.

Props can be excellent inspiration for frozen action gestures, and add context to the drawings:

- Catching a football
- Pounding a hammer
- Swinging a tennis racket
- Throwing a boomerang
- Throwing a discus
- Throwing a Frisbee
- Wielding a toy sword

Rope is a great prop to show muscle tension. Tie one end to the base of your model stand at the beginning of the class. Pull on the rope from a standing, kneeling, or sitting position. Experiment to find the most comfortable grip, so you can hold this pose longer. Poses can also be done with an untethered piece of rope, holding one end in each hand and stretching.

A pole is a very versatile prop. It can be used to simulate a variety of actions:

- Digging with a shovel
- Rowing a boat or paddling a canoe
- Shooting a goal with a hockey stick
- Spearing a fish
- Steering a Venetian gondola
- Swinging a baseball bat
- Swinging a golf club
- Throwing a spear (standing or kneeling)
- Wielding a lance

An umbrella can be used as a prop, but be careful of any overhead lighting when opening it.

You can either bring actual props, or just imagine using them. Imagining even ordinary actions can make interesting gestures.

- Changing a light bulb
- Reaching on the top shelf
- Sweeping the floor

Animators like very short poses. A figure drawing class in an animation program might start with 15-second poses. Poses this short are easy to hold, but you have to quickly think of your next pose. If you are asked to do 15-second poses for 10 minutes, you need to think of 40 poses. If you repeat a pose, rotate your body 90 or 180 degrees, so the artist will have to draw a very different perspective of the pose.

Another idea for quick gestures is sequential motion. This means breaking an action down into four or five components. Let's take swinging a baseball bat, for example. Start by holding the bat behind your shoulder for 15 seconds. Then swing the bat slightly forward and hold it there for 15 seconds. Next, swing forward a bit more and hold for 15 seconds. Finally, complete the swing and hold it for 15 seconds.

A very advanced variation of gesture poses is continuous motion. Tali Farchi, who is both an artist and an art model in The Netherlands, explains how she uses this concept:

> A major part of my work is the multimedia show Mo(ve)ment, which is actually drawing a dance and capturing the movement in the moment. Now when I model I do something that is a bit out of the ordinary. I pose in motion with music—I sort of dance as I am modeling. In doing so I repeat the movement in the dance so that the artists can come back to the same pose again and again. It makes for very fast drawing, but I do give a chance to concentrate on a single pose within the movement. These sessions are exhausting to the artist and to me, but very interesting.

Gesture poses can be a lot of fun. Be creative and show some energy.

The significance of gesture drawings

For many artists, gesture sketching is simply a warm-up exercise to help "loosen" their drawings. An emphasis on precision can result in a stiff drawing style. With 30-second gestures, there is no chance of capturing precise details, so the focus is on the overall flow of the pose.

For other artists, gestures are a key component of all drawings. In fact, "Gesture is the single most important element in the drawing," according to veteran animation professional Glenn Vilppu.[7.1]

Toronto-based artist Rie Shibazaki shares this view:

> Gesture drawing is a great way to hone the skill of seeing the entire pose quickly and then being able to get the entire pose down from head to toe as quickly and as accurately as possible. It is a good way to train to draw the entire line of action first, analyze proportional and positional relationships involving the whole body, and then slowly build up detail as time progresses.
>
> It really forces one to stay away from part-to-part drawing—like starting from the head, then shoulders, and then chest without planning for other body parts—which can cause proportion and positioning problems later on. I am sure you have seen drawings that are pretty good on the whole but are missing feet or hands because the artists did not plan out the drawing initially through jotting down the entire pose.
>
> The same method can be applied to longer poses and as a result, it produces very accurate proportions from the first minute into the pose. It's rather alarming to notice 30 minutes into an hour-long pose that the drawing is not proportionally correct because you started at the head and then worked your way down. Or realize that you don't have enough room for an out-stretched hand because you started too high up.

Some classes don't include any gesture poses. In animation programs, capturing extremely short poses is considered a core skill. In my experience, most figure drawing sessions fall somewhere in the middle, with one to three minute gesture poses being common.

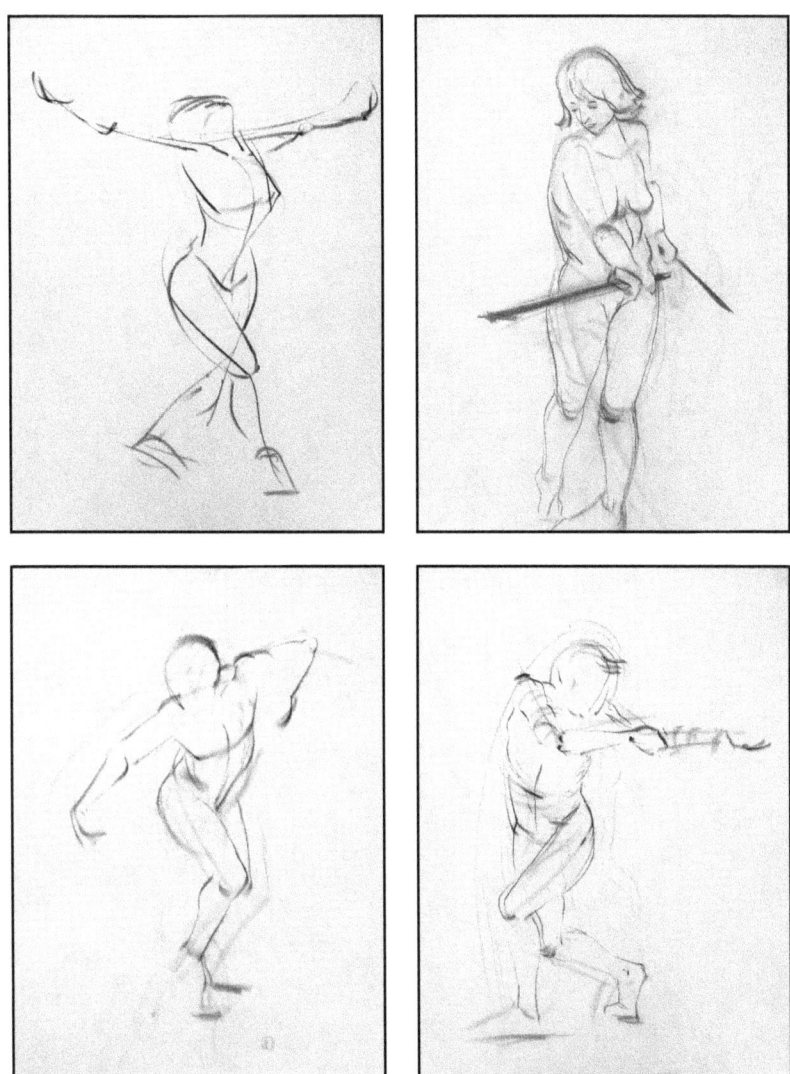

© 2007 Rie Shibazaki. Gesture sketches. Nupastel on newsprint. Top-left: 30 seconds; Top-right: 2 minutes; Bottom: 1 minute each.

Chapter 8

What Makes an Interesting Pose?

As art models, we must not lose sight of our purpose, which is to inspire and support the artist.

Throughout the years I have been modeling, I have always been curious about what makes artists tick. Where do they find inspiration? What is their process? The most fulfilling modeling experiences for me have been when it feels like a collaboration—a joint creative effort. The more in tune I am with how artists think, the better I can support them as a model.

To satisfy this curiosity, I have interviewed a variety of figurative artists. One of the core questions I asked was, "What makes an interesting pose?" Some of the responses to that question are below. The full interviews can be found at: www.artist-perspectives.com.

Expression. If it's got some kind of expression it's a good pose. You don't need a face visible for a body to express emotion.
— Felix Eddy

What interests me is the challenge of seizing an instant that reveals something about the life of the subject. It's all about relationships. How is the subject relating to the artist? To the viewer? To their surroundings? A good model is an actor really, experiencing a moment of truth. — John Crowther

I am often attracted to subtle poses emphasizing the vulnerability, emotionality or "humanness" of the human form.
— Antoine de Villiers

Good lighting, tastefulness, mechanics (what the body can do), environment, props (I often use them for symbols), expression (facial and otherwise), and body language.
— Joseph Larkin

There is so much that can make a captivating pose, such as energy, mood, dynamics, and lighting, but what I think makes a great pose is a model who is confident and comfortable while modeling. What I also look for in a figure model is a real and everyday person, flaws and all. — Douglas Pexa

I am torn between dramatic, twisted poses and very classical feeling poses. — Brian Bednarek

What I look for in a pose is that emotional expression. I don't particularly care if it is a male or female, dressed or nude. I want to capture the psychological state as expressed in the physical.
— Terry Rafferty

Things like curves that show muscles, folds, and overlapping make a pose interesting to work with, and eventually give me that sudden idea of something I want to make. — I.T. Hammar

The beauty and grace of the human form is emphasized with each twist and bend. — Art Krummel

A captivating pose would include proper lighting and well placed shadows. — Aletheia Rio

Chapter 9

Researching Poses

Master works

A great source of ideas for poses is to look at works of famous artists. You don't need to be an art history major; my knowledge of the topic is very shallow. Just peruse the art section of the library and discover interesting poses from classic works of art.

Explore the works of old masters:

- Giotto di Bondone (1267-1337)
- Andrea Mantegna (1431-1503)
- Sandro Botticelli (1445-1510)
- Luca Signorelli (1445-1523)
- Michelangelo (1475-1564)
- Caravaggio (1571-1610)
- Peter Paul Rubens (1577-1640)
- Rembrandt (1606-1669)

Or look at the works of more recent artists:

- Pierre Paul Prud'hon (1758-1823)
- Théodore Géricault (1791-1824)
- Eugène Delacroix (1798-1863)
- Auguste Rodin (1840-1917)
- Thomas Eakins (1844-1916)
- John Singer Sargent (1856-1925)
- Henri Matisse (1869-1954)
- Maxfield Parrish (1870-1966)
- Paul Cadmus (1904-1999)

The list goes on and on.

You could save yourself a trip to the library by starting with a Google image search (images.google.com). Search any above-mentioned artist and you will get pages of image results.

It is interesting how artists will interpret a pose. They may see something other than what the model has in mind. I once did a reclining pose based on the painting Lament for Icarus by Herbert James Draper. The instructor in the class commented on how the pose reminded him of Géricault's painting, The Raft of the Medusa.

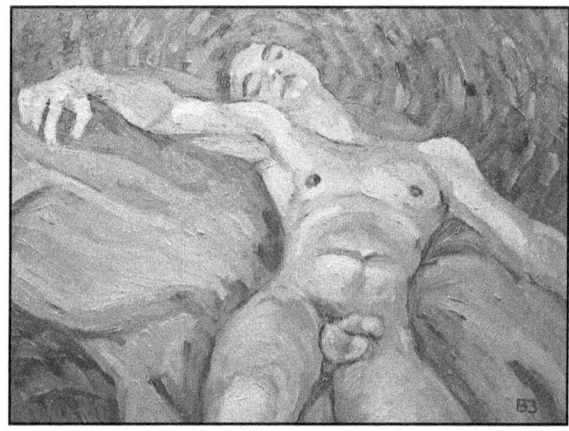

© 2003 Brian Bednarek. Acrylic painting.
This pose was based on a painting called
Lament for Icarus by Herbert James Draper.

Figure drawing books

Figure drawing instruction guides contain sample drawings which may give you some ideas for poses. These books also provide insights into the figure drawing process and the challenges faced by art students. Browse the figure drawing books in the library or the Art Techniques section of a local bookstore to find books with poses that appeal to you. Some figure drawing books include:

- Drawing the Male Nude by Giovanni Civardi
- Drawing the Female Nude by Giovanni Civardi
- Spirit of the Pose by Karl Gnass
- The Art of Figure Drawing by Clem Robins
- The Artist's Complete Guide to Figure Drawing by Anthony Ryder

Drawing reference photos

There are also books containing reference photographs of figure models in various poses. Examples include:

- Art Models: Life Nudes for Drawing, Painting, and Sculpting by Maureen and Douglas Johnson. This is the first book in a series. www.livemodelbooks.com

- Virtual Pose: The Ultimate Visual Reference Series for Drawing the Human Figure by Mario Henri Chakkour. This is also the first in a series. www.virtualpose.net

These sources can get your started, but you don't need to be a slave to them. With some creativity and practice, you'll develop a repertoire that you are comfortable with. But even seasoned models want to mix things up with new poses to keep it interesting for themselves and for their clients.

Practice

Practice modeling at home. Pose in front of a mirror, so you can see how the poses look. You could also take photos so you can review them afterwards. Set up a digital camera on a tripod. Frame the shot wide enough to include standing, sitting, and reclining poses. Most cameras have a self-timer, but this requires running back and forth to reset the timer after each pose. A remote control is more convenient.

Practice a set of 10 one-minute gestures. Count the seconds in your head and move from one pose immediately to the next.

Experiment with longer poses. Set your timer for 20 minutes. It's better to break a grueling pose at home and erase it from your repertoire than to endure it in a classroom.

Once you know how your poses look and how long you can hold them, you can choose poses intelligently when you're in the classroom.

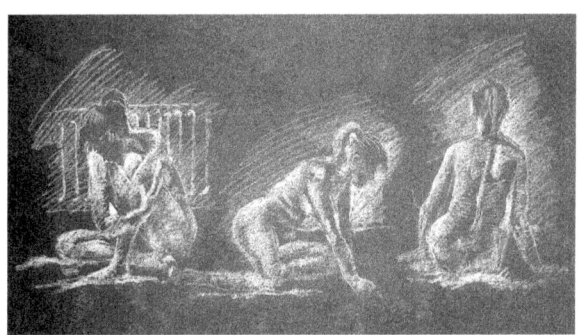

© 2005 Ronald Eyre. Three ten minute poses.
White pastel pencil on black pastel paper.

Chapter 10

Costume Modeling

So far, the focus of this book has been on nude figure modeling. However, there is also demand for art models in costume. Some schools pay a slightly higher rate for models with interesting wardrobes, to offset the cost of purchasing, cleaning, and repairing the attire.

Costume modeling is most common in illustration classes and animation workshops. A costume could be vintage fashion from a bygone era, traditional ethnic dress, a uniform, or something more theatrical. The client may simply be interested in the aesthetics of a costume.

Other clients want a specific character from history, literature, comics, etc. Character models, like actors, should "become" the character and pose authentically. Queen Elizabeth poses would be refined, elegant, and regal. Spiderman would be agile and dynamic.

Jennifer Fabos Patton has been an art model for nearly 20 years. I asked her to tell us about her costume modeling experience.

What kind of costumes do you model in?

It depends on the client. At Cal Arts I work for the animation department and they like all kinds of costumes: characters, strange wigs, glasses, shoes, and stockings. Sometimes the wackier, the better. When I work for the animation studios, they like comic book character costumes like Danger Girl, Cat Woman, and Matrix, or something kind of sexy like burlesque, Egyptian, or sexy sci-fi girl. Painters like more classic things like peasant women, Renaissance, Greek, and Victorian.

One of the most asked questions I get about all the costumes is where I get them and where do I keep them all. I collect little knick-knacks for the costumes all the time. I put the costumes together myself. I have literally hundreds of costumes. Somebody may ask me which costume I want to do. It is easier if they just tell me what they are looking for. I get a little flustered tying to remember them all. I usually say, "Just pick something you would like to see," and I probably have it or can come up with it. Cat Woman, Tank Girl, and a nun were requests. I didn't have those specifically, but I put them together easily. I had everything already for all three. I even amazed myself because the costumes turned out so good. They have been asking for them again and telling people how good they are.

Which costumes are most often requested?

Cowgirl, Victorian, Egyptian, belly dancer, punk, nurse, and Marie Antoinette. Funny thing is, the popularity will go in phases. Different people will start asking for the same thing and I don't think they know others are asking for it. It's like it's in the air. It could have something to do with movies, popular TV shows, or things that are happening in the world.

Each model has their own style with the costumes. My friend Marissa is around the same age as me, but has more of a soul in the Old West and does really authentic looking cowgirls, Calamity Jane, and Indians. She also has an Amelia Earhart costume.

Another good friend, Sara, makes up her own characters. Some are in the circus. Some are from other parts of the world, like Mongolia. She usually gives them names too and sometimes if we are doing pairs—two models hired to pose together—she will even dress me as the character's friend. The costumes are amazing, and she puts so much detail into them.

Which types of sessions most commonly request costume models: drawing, painting, or photography?

Drawing and Painting. In drawing classes they are typically doing faster poses, but sometimes longer poses when they are working on more detail. The painting classes are doing one long pose and trying to get a good painting out of it.

How many costume changes are typical in a session?

Typically just one. Occasionally two or three in an all-day drawing class (six hours), but these would be for quick poses.

What percentage of your bookings is for costume?

Well, when I started I didn't do that many costumes. Through the years I have been doing more and more. I believe it is because of the popularity with animation and the entertainment industry. They want more characters and costume models, action poses, and models doing things. Props can be handy for that too. So now I probably do more than 50% in costume. Maybe something like 60%.

Thanks, Jen, for sharing your experience.

Chapter 11

Finding Work

Guilds and associations

If you live in one of the few areas that has a models guild, this can be a great resource for finding modeling jobs. The Bay Area Models Guild in northern California serves as a booking agency. DFW Art Models (serving the Dallas area) and The Figure Models Guild of Washington, D.C. provide referrals. The Register of Artists' Models serves the United Kingdom.

Art classes

Figure Drawing, sometimes called Life Drawing, is part of the core curriculum for studio art majors at most art schools, colleges, and universities. Figure painting and figure sculpture classes also use models. Contact the art department and ask who books the models. Sometimes there is a model coordinator for the department. In other cases, the instructors book their own models.

While figure drawing classes are usually conducted with nude models, this is not always the case. There are figure drawing classes for teenage students—some use nude models while others ask the model to wear swim attire. I have experienced both situations. I must admit that when I was booked to model nude for high school students, I was somewhat doubtful of their maturity level, but I was pleasantly surprised. They were well behaved, and serious about their art. I assume that at least a few of them were preparing portfolios to apply for admission to art colleges.

Brigham Young University, which is owned by the Mormon

church, does not use nude models. According to Utah-based art model Ben Miller, "BYU's female models wear skin-tight body suits provided by the school. Their male models wear Speedos."[11.1] When the model is not nude, the course description may refer to a "draped" model.

Models in portrait classes remain clothed, since the students are only drawing the model's head.

Photography classes generally use clothed models. However, photography lighting workshops sometimes use a nude model, and students may use nude models for their assignments.

Other sources of work

Aside from a formal art class, there are other formats in which a model will be hired to pose for a group of artists.

Uninstructed workshops are offered by schools and other organizations. Similarly, an artist may host an open studio, sharing the cost of hiring a model with other artists.

Individual artists hire models to pose privately. In this case, the artist usually has a specific concept in mind, and will direct the model. Collaborating with a professional artist can be the most fulfilling of art modeling experiences. The work takes on new significance when you consider that the finished artwork could be published, exhibited in a gallery, or end up in a museum or private collection. I am aware that one painting of me was sold to a doctor in Italy.

Animation studios also hire figure models from time to time. While computer graphics are heavily used by this industry, fundamental artistic skills are still relevant. Drawing sessions for animators will generally focus on shorter, dynamic poses.

Web sources to find modeling gigs:

www.craigslist.org
Ads seeking models are usually posted in the Gigs section, under the Creative or Talent subcategories.

www.modelmayhem.com
Model Mayhem was originally a site for models to connect with photographers and that is still its core constituency. However, the site now includes a membership category called Artist/Painter.

www.onemodelplace.com
This site is similar to Model Mayhem in its scope.

figuredrawing.meetup.com
Meetup calls itself "the world's largest network of local groups." There are numerous figure drawing groups on this site.

www.artmod.org
Based in the U.K., but artists and models from anywhere can create a profile. Work notices are posted, and emailed to members. Messages can also be sent to individual members from their profile, but the search function makes it difficult to find someone in a specific area.

www.thegreatnude.tv
This feature of the Community section was "coming soon" as of press time: "Models who are Members can connect with artists and photographers who are hiring models."

These resources will help you get started. Once you become active in the local art community, you will become aware of more opportunities. And once you develop a reputation as a creative and dependable model, you will get more repeat bookings and referrals. After modeling for a painting class at a local college, the instructor recommended me to the model coordinator at another art school. I have received ongoing bookings as a result of that one recommendation.

Sporadic work

Very few people work full time as an art model. Aside from the physical strain, it is difficult to piece together enough jobs to work full time. For example, working an eight-hour day might entail working a three-hour class in the morning, a three-hour class at another location in the afternoon, and a two-hour session at another location in the evening. Ultimately, supply and demand is a major factor in the frequency of work.

In most figure drawing classes, models are rotated over the term. Often male and female models are alternately booked.

Each model brings something different in terms of poses and body type. If students drew only one model for an entire semester, they'd only practice drawing one type of body, rather than learning how to draw *any* body. Rotating the models constantly challenges the artists to draw something slightly unfamiliar.

That said, instructors tend to request models they like. A sought-after model is dependable, able to hold still, and chooses interesting poses. However, there are subjective factors as well. Nancy Lilly explains:

> I was an art student, I did a bit of teaching, I ran an art gallery office, and I modeled for 18 years. But when I put on my clothes and sat down behind the desk as a model manager, I learned a lot more about how things really work. I thought that to be a good, dependable, knowledgeable, hard-working model was it. Let me tell you, so many of the faculty—plus artists and workshop leaders—view the model so much more subjectively

than I ever knew. It doesn't mean that the rules should be tossed out the window, but it does mean that no matter how great an individual model is, there will be a teacher or artist who thinks that model should be banned from posing. And no matter how 'bad' a model is, there will be an artist who thinks that model is the very best.

How much money do art models earn?

Model rates vary regionally. As of this writing in March 2009, art models in Los Angeles generally earn between $20 and $25 per hour, although some community colleges pay less.

According to the Bay Area Models Guild website, model rates range from $25 per hour in San Francisco and Oakland, to $52 per hour in San Jose, Sonoma, and Napa Valley. The Guild has a three-hour minimum booking.[11.2]

The DFW Art Models website states that models in the Dallas area earn $15 to $20 per hour. But, "if an artist needs a model to shoot for photo reference only to use for a painting or a sculpture, the going rate is" $30 to $50 per hour if the model is clothed, or $50 to $75 per hour if the model is nude.[11.3] See Chapter 17, Photography, for more on reference photography.

According to the book Modeling Life, published in 2006, models in Portland, Oregon earn $8.50 to $10 per hour.[11.4]

Some organizations pay models as contractors and send a Form 1099, if earnings exceed $600 in the calendar year. The model is responsible for all tax filings. They may ask you to submit an invoice for your fees, or they may have their own form. Other organizations pay the model as an employee. The model submits a timecard and receives a payroll check with taxes withheld. In this case the model is sent a Form W2 at the end of the year.

Keep accurate records, as some bureaucracies are not very efficient at paying their bills. It doesn't matter if you use an Excel spreadsheet or a piece of lined paper, but record every modeling session and the amount you earned. Update the record when you receive the payment for that session. If you aren't paid after a couple of weeks, or within the normal agreed turnaround time with that client, then you need to inquire about the status.

As a contractor, the revenue you receive from your clients, minus your business expenses, equals net earnings. As a sole proprietorship, you'll most likely report this to the IRS on Schedule C along with Form 1040. If your earnings are significant, you may have to pay estimated taxes every quarter. Contractors should keep mileage records, as transportation to visit clients may be a deductible expense.

The forms mentioned in this section pertain to the United States; obviously they will vary in other countries. I raise these as matters for your awareness, not as tax advice. Consult a CPA or licensed tax professional if you need help with taxes.

Some schools have bureaucratic hiring procedures, including verifying employment with current and past employers. This seems ridiculous for a part-time modeling job, and can be a concern for models who wish to keep their modeling work separate from their day job.

Chapter 12

Security Concerns

It is important to be vigilant about bookings, whether for drawing, painting, or photography. Be especially careful about one-on-one bookings. If contacted by an unfamiliar artist, ask some questions to make sure the client is legitimate. If he or she was referred to you, verify with the referring person.

The anonymous nature of online resources, such as Craigslist, calls for added caution. I have been booked for some art classes by responding to Craigslist ads, but there are also some dubious ads on there. Likewise, models who have their own websites need to carefully vet the inquiries received through that channel.

For a one-on-one booking, it can be reassuring if the prospective client has a professional website with a portfolio of artwork. If not, ask to see samples of his or her work, and/or ask for references. Art gallery representation is another sign of legitimacy.

Although the preponderance of bookings are legitimate, there are occasionally those which are not—even to the point of being dangerous. As an art student, art model, and model manager, Nancy Lilly has a wealth of experience spanning more than 50 years. The stories she recalls for us vividly demonstrate the need to be careful and alert:

> A number of dicey things have happened at schools. Faculty should be aware and protective of the model's

vulnerability, but often they are either totally focused on the class and teaching situation, or ignorant—to be honest.

- Many years ago, a student decided the model was the epitome of sexual evil. He jumped onto the model stand and tried to choke her.

- A "looky-loo" who had come into the class waited in his car at the bottom of the hill to try to follow the model home—not for the best of reasons. Luckily the model picked up on it, came back to the school, and contacted Security. The guy left real quick!

- Fifteen or 20 years ago, a guy wandered through the building, looking in on classes. He had a jacket over his arm. In one studio, a student noticed light reflecting from something under the jacket. The guy was videotaping the models. The student yelled a warning. A major chase ensued. The guy was chased through the building and outside. Police were called and a helicopter followed the chase. A security guard fell on the hill and broke his leg. The guy fell and dropped the camera, but kept running and was able to get away in the hills. We got the camera. He had been focusing on the models' crotches, and had been doing this in several classes. The teachers were oblivious. Sheesh! A year later, I witnessed the burning of the tape. The guy was not found, no one was chastised; it was forgotten in the overall scheme of things.

- A guy was calling models, using other models as references. He was sending models to addresses that didn't exist. Luckily, the models had sense enough to leave, rather than get out of their cars and wander around. It was creepy. I tried to track him down with phone numbers and such, and put the word out to all the models to beware. I don't know where he got the first model's name, but when he would call a model who refused him, he would use their name for a reference. It was weird.

- Another time a model showed up at school. She had been booked for a non-existent class in a room number that did not exist.

- There have been, of course, many situations where a model would accept a booking and go to a supposedly legitimate job and have some S.O.B. expect [sexual services]. And then you hope that you will get out physically unscathed. Been there… Done that.

These stories are the exception, not the rule. But they are good examples of occasional bad situations that do occur, and demonstrate the need for models to be alert.

Chapter 13

Faculty Guide to Working With Models

This chapter may be downloaded in PDF format for free at www.
artmodelbook.com. Permission is granted to distribute the chapter in
its entirety, without changes, via email or hardcopy.

The instructor is in charge of the class, and has a primary
responsibility of teaching the students. However, when models
are used, the instructor has the added responsibility to understand
and comply with standard practices. This applies to leaders of
uninstructed workshops as well.

Brief the model at the beginning of the class. Explain what
you are covering in the lesson. Models are usually expected to
choose their own poses. If they understand your teaching goals,
they will be better informed in their choice of poses. If you are
teaching how to draw feet, the poses will prominently feature
the feet. If you are teaching about tone, the model will be more
aware of shadows. If your model is experienced—or has read
this book—he or she will understand common art terms like
foreshortening and negative space. If not, be patient and explain
what you need.

The instructor specifies the duration of poses. In a figure drawing
class, it is common to open with very short gestures, gradually
working up to longer, more relaxed poses.

**Standard practice allows the model a five-minute break
after 20 to 25 minutes of posing.** Do not expect a model to
pose for more than 25 minutes unless the model agreed before
the pose began. Reclining poses tend to be the easiest to hold,
and the model may be willing to hold such a pose for longer
than the standard limit.

Be aware that some poses are more strenuous than others. The more dynamic poses can be held only a short time. Asking a model to repeat a gesture pose for 25 minutes is probably unrealistic. However, some compromise may be possible. If the pose can be modified to provide more support and balance, it may be close enough for your objectives. Also, it might be possible to hold the pose in a series of shorter increments. Be reasonable in the trade off between duration and difficulty.

Even relatively relaxed poses can cause physical strain. Models frequently experience a hand or foot falling asleep, a temporary peripheral nerve disorder known in medical terms as mononeuropathy. Prolonged pressure on a nerve can damage it.[13.1] Breaks are necessary to allow the model to rest and recover.

The following must be cleared with the models in advance:
- Figure models working together on the same stand.
- Male and female models posing nude in same studio.

No cameras are allowed in the studio. Photos and videos are prohibited, unless specific permission has been given and releases have been signed. If photos are necessary, such as to aid in repositioning the model for a multiple-day pose, make sure to state this requirement prior to booking the model. This can be a condition of accepting the job. Some models will be comfortable with this, while others may choose to turn down a job with such a condition.

Do not touch the model without permission. To point out lighting or anatomy features, a laser pointer is advised— except near the eyes. If the model will be resuming a pose after a break, it may be necessary to mark the pose with masking tape. Ask the model if he or she would like help taping pose. Some may appreciate the assistance while it may make others uncomfortable.

No visitors or tours are allowed to enter the studio when a model is posing nude or semi-nude without permission from both the instructor and the model. The model must be given the option to put on a robe and take a break while visitors go through. See also Chapter 12, Security Concerns.

Model stands are for the use of models and for set-ups designated by faculty, not for student use as an easel substitute, picnic table, etc.

Models should be supplied with fans or space heaters as necessary and given a clean environment in which to work.

Safety has priority before aesthetics. A model should not be expected to pose in an uncomfortable or potentially dangerous situation, such as an unstable support or on top of a ladder. Be sure that lights and any props are stable and balanced.

If you would like something out of the ordinary, it should be cleared with the model when the booking is made. Nancy Lilly says it best: "Some models can handle a difficult standing pose for three hours; some cannot. Some models are not afraid of heights; some are. Some models are comfortable working closely with other models; some are not. The needs of your classes are the priority, and planning ahead will enable you to have what you need."

Problems with models should be dealt with privately, not in front of the class. Sometimes a model's abilities and personality fit well in one class, but not in another. If a model does not hold poses well, is careless about break times, or is unprofessional in any way, please either point out the problem to the model or notify the model coordinator.

Chapter 14

Interview with a Model Booker:
Wendy McClay-Triplett

Wendy McClay-Triplett is Manager of Models and Props at Art Center College of Design in Pasadena, California. Her department books models for 75 to 100 sessions per week. As someone in the eye of the storm, she has seen it all. In this interview, she shares some insights from the perspective of hiring models for college classes.

What are the most common complaints you hear from instructors?

The model is *late*. That is always number one: late arrival to the beginning of a class, as well as late arrival back to class after a break. This is the number one reason why a model will not be requested again.

What traits or skills are most requested by instructors?

Traits
Reliability. Honestly this is the most important thing above all else. If you are not reliable you will never get booked a second time nor will you receive any referrals.

Skills
Creativity coupled with a variety of poses and the ability to hold them. Listen to what the instructor is teaching and pose to fit the needs of the class. This will get a model requested repeatedly by certain instructors. Showing interest in the needs of the class is very simple. Arrive early and make contact with the instructor

before the class begins. Ask questions about what they need for that assignment. Also instead of leaving the class on every break or when the teacher is lecturing, sit in the room and listen to the lectures that the teachers give. This will give the model insight on what the class is doing and how the model can inspire with their next set of poses.

I bet you have some good advice on finding work, since you hire a lot of art models.

Models often get a bad rap for professionalism. The reason is that some tend to forget that even though modeling is creative and artistic, that places such as the college I work for expect a model to be able to leave a clear, coherent telephone message or write a clear e-mail when contacting my office about modeling work. My procedure for the hiring of new models is that the model contacts my office, either by phone or e-mail, and requests a packet of model information. I can send this information in the regular mail, although we prefer to send the entire packet via e-mail to save resources.

The model then has the responsibility to read through the information provided and return certain forms and photos to me so that I can create a file for them. I would say that 50% of the applications I get are incomplete. They are missing necessary forms, the forms are not completed, the photos submitted are not what was asked for, etc.

Professionalism has to start with the first contact. This will establish if this person seems responsible enough to be here on time and follow directions.

How do you decide whom to hire?

I book models based on faculty requests and direction. Many faculty members have their favorite models who are requested every single term. When the direction of the class is as simple as male figure or female figure, I book based on responsibility and professionalism. My requests vary a great deal from class to class. Sometimes I will need a model with great planes of the head or a great torso, or a Cleopatra costume, or an action gesture model. Anything and everything comes across my desk. I have heard it all, I think...

What causes an application to go in the circular file?

Denied applications are those which are incomplete, or models who never follow up on their availability after applying.

What criteria are used to decide which models are booked regularly, and which are used to fill in?

I currently have approximately 200 models on file here at Art Center. I would estimate that less than 25% of those 200 work with some regularity—three to more than 40 hours per month. These would be models who have established themselves with certain teachers and are requested every term for classes. The other 75% fall into several different categories. These are only a few:

- Models who have limited availability due to other careers or school;
- Untested Models who have not worked here before nor have any references or recommendations from other models or faculty;
- Models with specific looks—if a faculty member wants a heavy set female figure or a muscular Asian male, I may only have one or two on file, and anyone else would not be a suitable replacement;
- New models with no experience would be called last in the case of a last minute cancellation.

Professionalism is what gets you hired back on a repeat basis.

Models who are late and/or unreliable, who are always complaining or whining, who have no energy on the model stand, who talk while modeling on the stand or who have a poor attitude in the class will not be asked back to model.

Aside from dependability, what else makes a positive impression?

Preparedness. The most prepared models have a modeling bag in their car. Many models also have miscellaneous costumes or costume pieces in their car including hats and high heels, just to be prepared for anything. I love a well-prepared model!

Thanks for sharing your perspective, Wendy.

Chapter 15

Interview with a Male Model: David R. Quammen

David R. Quammen is an art model, founder of the Figure Models Guild of Washington D.C., and a co-director of MOCA DC/ A+M Galleries. My interview with him was originally published on Artist-Perspectives.com.

How long have you been an art model?

I started modeling on Halloween Day 2000.

There must be many thousands of drawings and paintings of you. Does it ever concern you that your likeness may be recognized by someone you know?

I don't have any concerns about people who may recognize me in an artists rendering. I think that Western mores regarding nudity are a bit over done and a bit prudish. For those who believe in God, we are supposedly made in His image. If that is fact, then it strikes me as hypocritical to be ashamed of His image when it is presented in an artistic endeavor.

What qualifications does one need to model professionally?

There are several, but there are some minimum standards. I consider a model to be a tool for the instructor, a template for the artist, and an inspiration to the process. As a tool for the instructor, the model can help by showing up early to find out what is being covered that day. If it is a new class, then complex poses would be inappropriate. If the lesson were on negative space, then the poses should be those where everyone in the class can have at least some minimal view showing negative space.

As a template for the artist, the model should take care to remain in the same position during the pose, not move parts of the body, or if necessary, tell the class that, for example the right arm is asleep and will be moved in one minute, while leaving the rest of the pose intact. If a long pose, the model should take a pose that could be held for more than 20 minutes at a time. Based on discussions with many artists and teachers, the longer the model is in the pose, the greater the potential creativity is instilled in the artist, thus a better result.

As an inspiration to the process, some models have a natural presence, which, all else being equal, helps the pose to be inspirational. Models should be aware of their own limitations for endurance, or whether or not they look good in some poses. For every given body type—even a 10 on the good-looking scale—there are some poses that just don't look right. Facial expressions are also important. For example, a smile would look absurd in a pose that suggests drama or stress.

Do you have a standard repertoire of poses or do you mostly look for direction from the artists or instructor?

When I first started modeling, there were no guides available. Over time, I took digital pictures of poses done by famous artists, as well as from the classics. I reduced them to one inch then organized them in categories of standing, seated and reclining; these are now in a pose guide that I give to models, whether new or experienced, for reference until they gain enough experience to develop their own poses. I try to avoid doing the same poses all the time, but I do have a few standard guidelines. For example, I believe that modeling begins when the model gets to the model stand. Avoid distracting the class if the teacher is speaking to them. If the session starts with a series of short gesture poses, I treat it as a dance, knowing in advance what pose I'll do next, make a smooth transition then allow a few seconds before starting the count. I always count short poses in my head, since I believe that a timer is disruptive and detracts from a smooth transition from one pose to the next.

What constitutes an interesting pose? What makes a pose compelling for an artist?

This is a tough question, and differs from artist to artist. Some prefer poses with a lot of drama, others like a more natural pose. Even natural poses can have a lot of movement, so I try to take poses with a lot of action, or that suggest something realistic that is recognizable.

How do you sustain long poses without moving?

First I make sure the pose has a good balance. When I'm settled into it, I find two or three points for reference then find something to concentrate on. I'm fairly fit, so I check that these reference points are where they should be. I've done a lot of planning while modeling, and let my mind go to work on whatever it is at the time.

Who do you model for?

I've modeled for just about every school and group in the greater Washington D.C. area, and for quite a few artists privately. I'm rather aggressive, so when I found that I enjoyed it, I sought out every place I could.

Is the demand for male and female art models equal?

There's a greater demand for female models than males, although there are more male than female models who can model during the day. A lot of the female models are in college, which limits their daytime availability. Even if there were an equal number with an equal availability, I think the demand would be higher for female models than male. There are several reasons for this, including that society is more accepting of female nudes in the arts, that society in general has a dim view of the male nude, and that a lot of males seem to be homophobic.

Are there many male art models? Do you find a supply and demand imbalance (too many or not enough)?

In the D.C. area, there are definitely more male models than females. All the places I model ask if I can send some female models.

What type of modeling gigs do you like best?

I prefer modeling for organized groups that meet on a regular basis, or for the schools with a high ratio of adult students. Generally, the artists are more serious about their art and have a greater respect for the model.

What type of jobs do you try to avoid?

Schools with students who are taking art classes more because they are required for web-related curricula; they tend to be less interested in their art, and are thus less attentive and more prone to joke around and disrupt the concentration in the class.

What was your most fulfilling modeling experience?

There have been several instances where the class applauded after some rigorous poses. It helps to know the effort is appreciated.

And your worst experience?

While modeling for a class where the teacher was out of the room reviewing students as part of the final evaluation, three students were talking, disturbing the class and irritating me as the pose was particularly difficult and I wasn't taking a break. I finally told them to shut up or I'd leave. It was the first of three sessions, and the class told the teacher that I was right; they never spoke again during that or the remaining two nights.

What advice do you have for people interested in modeling for artists?

If you're really interested in being a professional model, treat it like anything else that you might enjoy doing. Learn the ropes and respect that those you are modeling for are spending their time and money to learn or practice their art, and you're a major part of the lesson.

You founded the Figure Models Guild in July of 2002. Why did you start this organization? What is its mission?

When I first started modeling, many artists told me that models wouldn't show up, would show up late and couldn't hold a pose even if they knew what one was. As I became more familiar with it, I discovered that the artist community was partially to blame because no organization trained models. The major source of new models was via ads in a local paper—if you agreed to take your clothes off, you were called a model and could get as many gigs and at the same rate of pay as those with years of experience. I saw problems on both sides of the easel, but it would be easier to work with the models for change than with the user community. Basically, I did it to make the model pool more dependable by making the models more professional.

The primary mission is to enhance the relationship between

artists and models. At this juncture, I have to say that the mission is being accomplished.

What does the Guild do to support its members?

First, I maintain a Model Registry that is given to all the schools, groups and individual artists who hire models. This includes the model's name, a headshot, physical description and other pertinent info, including how to contact them. I've put together what I call the Art of Modeling: A Handy Guide for Figure Models. This includes a two-page narrative covering the basics, and a pose guide of one inch images organized by standing, seated and reclining poses: 220 for the female, 208 for the male.

I also maintain a Figurative Arts Directory, listing places that use models. It includes address, contact information, nearest Metro station, how much they pay models, etc. There is a separate listing of open groups that's available on the web site for the guild.

What activities or events does the Guild sponsor?

The first Sunday of each month, we have a Model Meeting; the first hour is set aside to meet each other and discuss various issues in modeling. Artists are encouraged to attend this part of the meeting. Then models model and artists draw. It gives experienced models a chance to learn new poses. It also provides a venue for those interested in becoming a model, to see how artists work from the model and to try it themselves, if they choose. There is no pressure to model nude, and some have actually modeled clothed, or partially clothed. We also have open sessions on Monday and Wednesday nights from 7:00 to 10:00 p.m. Models are scheduled and paid for these, and artists pay a fee to attend. The Monday session uses two models, the first from 7:00 to 8:30, the second from 8:30 to 10:00. I try to schedule a male and female for these, which is shorter gesture to longer, 15 to 20 minute poses. The Wednesday session has one model, one pose for the session. Periodically, we schedule two models together for the long pose session.

We also have workshops, perhaps as a more concentrated training session for new models, or a two-model pose for two or three sessions.

What are some of your favorite art books?

My favorite art books are those with a lot of illustrations of the nude figure. An artist friend, for whom I've modeled often, has a lot of books that he graciously let me borrow, including one of Paul Cadmus, Pierre Paul Prud'hon (very similar style and technique), John Singer Sargent and a few others with a lot of inspirational poses. Also Kenneth Clark's The Nude: A Study in Ideal Form, and The Artist's Model: From Etty to Spencer. The latter is a book produced to accompany an exhibit held in 1999 in New York, London and Nottingham.

More recently, I've come to enjoy The Undressed Art: Why We Draw, by Peter Steinhart, an artist, naturalist and writer living in Palo Alto. Besides getting favorable reviews in the New York Times and Washington Post, Peter attended several sessions of the Figure Models Guild when it was first being organized. He told me then that he was writing a book about artists and models—little did I realize that I would end up being mentioned in his book. Aside from that, it is a good read.

You are a partner in the Museum of Contemporary Art in Washington, D.C. Tell me about what that organization does, and your role in it.

When I was starting the guild, Clark, the director of MOCA, let me use the gallery for organizing meetings, and was very supportive of the goal. It was an immediate success, and MOCA has been home to the Guild ever since. His guiding principle has been to provide a venue for innovative and undiscovered art and artists. Later, I founded A+M Galleries (Artist & Model), as a way to provide figurative artists a venue for their work. It's basically wall space in commercial lounges, but it has been well received. I was interested in finding a home base for it as well, so I approached Clark about hosting more exhibits. At that time, he was faced with operating the gallery by himself, so we decided to join forces and in January I became a co-director of MOCA DC/A+M Galleries. My role is to guarantee the rent each month, manage the day-to-day operations and organize shows. I've had to cut back on my modeling, but this new arrangement is a challenge that I really enjoy.

Thank you for sharing your experiences, Dave.

Chapter 16

Interview with a Female Model: Parker McPhinney

Parker McPhinney has been an art model for 22 years. In 1996 she produced a video documentary called Surrounded by Art: The Art Model's Perspective. The documentary is now available on DVD.

You have been modeling for 22 years. Approximately how many different schools have you modeled for in that time?

At least 40, maybe more. I stopped counting at one point.

This is sort of an obscure job. How did you get started?

I was living in San Diego when I started modeling. My girlfriends knew that I was 'starving' because I refused to do any job that wasn't connected to my acting goals. (I am a former actress.) So my girlfriend was supposed to pose for these nice English ladies who did watercolor. She was pregnant and couldn't keep the gig. She convinced me to go, telling me how lovely these ladies were. So I went. She was right; they were lovely, and one gentleman was with their group. They treated me like *gold*. I was a natural. I fell in love with it the very first day.

Which setting do you enjoy the most: do you prefer modeling for classes, artist groups, or individual artists?

I love them all. I just require respect. And I give that back. It's a marriage. You give and you take, with love.

What was your favorite modeling experience?

That's hard to answer. There are millions. But the greatest joy comes when you know the artist is engaged and loving what he is doing. That energy feeds you, and you then give even more. I think being present when someone makes a breakthrough in their work is very magical. I work a lot privately and some of the artists that I pose for then end up becoming friends. It's a joy to know you shared in the process of them achieving their creative goals.

Being on the set of *Star Trek* was pretty cool. That was a long time ago—but still very amazing.

The first time I ever posed at Disney studios, and I looked up and saw the prototype sculptures for all the cartoons I had watched as a kid in the 60's.

I also had the great joy to work one-on-one with *Peter Falk*. He's a great artist. I never would have dreamt that modeling would lead me to meet so many very talented people, known and unknown. But the greatest joy is just doing the work you love. And I love modeling.

You were a model on Star Trek?

Yes, I was Captain Picard's art model in the episode named, "A Matter of Perspective" on the Star Trek: The Next Generation series. The segment opened with him painting the model—me! On the set there was a huge effort to make me comfortable, and also to handle the nudity issues of TV. At first they wanted me to don pasties. That wasn't a good idea as far as I was concerned. It is never that way in a life drawing session. That would make it more Las Vegas. They did a soft focus. I think it was a back view. It's been 19 years. I do forget these details even if I was unwittingly making history. I think it can safely be said, a new precedent was created that day in TV, managing to have nudity on television without breaking any laws.

Have you had any bad experiences?

Very few. Once someone asked me to "take some playboy poses." This was in a group setting. I was very insulted and told him so. I almost left the booking on the spot, but I realized he was just a clueless guy looking for something that he wasn't going to find in *that* drawing session. I think it took a couple of hours before I calmed down about it. If I remember correctly he was asked to leave. It was a long time ago.

Have you ever felt unsafe? Do you have any advice for new female models about screening or safety?

Yes, I did have one time during a private booking when I realized I wasn't in the presence of someone who was mentally stable. You have to really screen people when you work privately. Ask for references. Ask what kind of work they do: the medium, the style. Who has worked for them before? What gallery represents them, or where do they show? In other words, find out if they are serious artists. Let others know when you go to a booking for someone privately that you've not established a relationship with—especially if you are female and they are male.

We had a period here in L.A. when someone got a model's list of numbers and was calling models making bookings at schools. The model would go and no one would be there! It was a scary thing, as he knew the 'language' of the job, and was sending models on wild goose chases. He disappeared and the calls stopped, but that spooked me for a while. You have to double-check things. You have to be smart. Get to know other models. Ask them for feedback on schools, teachers, and artists who run workshops. Know your environment. When you leave a classroom, be aware of your surroundings in the parking lots, etc. People *do* assume many things about us, just because we are nude in front of strangers.

Make clear the boundaries that you need to feel safe. My big thing now is *cell phones* being pulled out in classroom situations. The students of today were raised on them. They don't think before pulling them out. And there you are naked on the stand. They can take a photo and throw it on the Internet and you won't even know. I get very vocal with anyone I see pulling a cell phone out. They need to be educated on protocol and respecting the model when they are new at drawing the figure.

Which do you enjoy most, figure modeling for drawing, painting, or sculpting?

I really do love it all. I like that it's all mixed up. Sometimes working costume is the greatest joy. I create costumes and themes and I use storytelling by bringing a ton of props to work with. This is especially so with the animators. But some days I just want to move a lot, and so the drawing sessions where they want five-minute poses for five or six hours is just as much a joy. I am a person who needs to do many things, so modeling at the different schools and for various artists always allows that. Every school or person has different needs. I can stand for six hours in the same pose if I have to, but doing *only* that wouldn't be as exciting for me. That's why I love being a self-employed person. It's always changing day to day—it's never the same. One day: long pose. Next day: costumes. Third day might be gestures all day. Fourth day might be working with someone who is doing a long study of the same pose for weeks. Every day is a new situation. One has to be flexible to get a lot of work.

Tell me about your experience with animation studios.

I have worked for all the studios—DreamWorks, Sony, Disney,

Warner Bros., the animation union—at various times, and continue to work for them now and then. Also most of the private schools have an animation department. Basically it depends on the teacher's focus, be it figure, storytelling, or both. Sometimes it requires costumes with themes. But all of them love and require quick poses—30 seconds, one, two, and three minutes—usually for the entire session, which tends to be two hours for the studios. If costume/theme is the order of the day, the poses are usually five to 10 minutes.

Have you done sculpture modeling?

Yes.

What's that experience like?

The same pose for weeks and weeks.

What do you think about during a long pose?

India. I've been there eight times. I run astrology charts in my head; I am also a professional astrologer. Sometimes I just focus on the breath. Sometimes I have a grand fantasy about what I would do if I won the lotto that week. I solve problems, and chant and come up with new creative projects for myself. And on some days, I struggle *not* to focus on how much pain I am in.

Tell me about costume modeling.

I get many jobs just because of the costumes I have created. I recently developed a "Queen of Hearts" costume. It took me a month of brainstorming to bring it all together—and some of that brainstorming was done on the model stand in pose! I have many costumes: 20's flapper, Spanish Horse Rider, Clown Jester, Asian Indian, 1800's, mermaid, etc. One is always adding to the collection. When I am shopping and see something that I think the artists will like, I buy it and build around a theme. I have even had costumes custom made. I am often checking out yard sales and second hand stores for ideas to create a new costume. It's part of the fun of being a model, and ensures that you'll continue to get work to build varied repertoire of costumes.

Have you modeled for photography?

In the beginning I modeled for photography. For the last 15 or so years I stopped. I no longer want to pose for the camera being nude, even though I have worked with some marvelous, internationally known photographers. I reached a point where I no longer wanted nude photos of myself floating around. You really never know where they are going to end up. You can't control it. I love the camera. Don't get me wrong. It's a great tool to make art with, but as I got older I made different choices. I figure there's enough of me out there already. Recently I did a shoot with someone I'd worked with in the late 80's and early 90's, but it was costumed. The camera is just like a person to me. You pose as if its lens is a human eye, which it is.

What kind of jobs would you avoid?

Any individual or group who doesn't respect the model, or just works you to death: ignores need for breaks, doesn't care about the room temperature, isn't protective of the model, etc. Anyone that doesn't pay the current rates, or takes an unreasonable amount of time to pay. I expect payment at the time of service with privates, and within two weeks for the schools. I stop working for any place that cancels me often. This is a big issue for me. I get booked months in advance, and turn down several jobs for the same day. If a school or person books me three months in advance and then cancels me two weeks before the job, I have not only lost out on that job, but I turned down half a dozen more! Since I don't cancel on them I ask for the same level of security I offer. Of course every now and then things happen, and classes get cancelled, but it should be that the model is paid if it is last minute. As a matter of fact, I tell every private they have to pay my full fee if I get less than one-week notice. Many schools already have that policy. I think *all* of them should.

Do you model full time?

Yes. And I should add that a 40-hour model week would kill you. I work about 30 to 35 hours a week modeling. Any more and I am ready to drop dead. It is very much physical labor. You have to recharge. Plus I do other things as well.

How do you promote yourself?

At this point—after 22 years of it—I don't really have to promote myself anymore. There are new teachers that come in and people recommend me, so I really don't have to go after jobs anymore. If I am working someplace and an artist I have never worked for asked for my card, I give it. That's about the level of promoting I do. I don't call artists asking or looking for work. It's a bit like expecting the plumber to call and ask if the pipes need repairing. I never wanted to put people on the spot. I think it's the southerner in me, not wanting to be rude.

When you produced Surrounded by Art, what was the most interesting thing you learned about art modeling?

How much they had to say. You see, we aren't supposed to talk on the model stand. Models are a group of people who have chosen a very unusual way to make a living, and they do many, many things in addition to being muses. I was not surprised that there were amazing stories of how they ended up on the model stand, just surprised that each and every model had an amazing story! It was very hard to edit. I wanted it to be three hours long. I also learned how much they wanted to have a voice, and I was thankful they trusted me and shared as openly as they did. They were raw and honest, just like we are on the stand. I am forever thankful to each and everyone who help tell the art models' story.

What advice would give someone interested in getting started as an art model?

Have a good car. Be professional from the start, on time, and ready to work hard. Go to the library and check out art books. Learn who is who. If a teacher says, "I need a Egon Schiele pose," you need to know who that is. Stand naked in front of a friend for an hour and don't move for 25 minutes at a time. See if you can do this. Then do 40 different one-minute poses and make sure they are all different. And then GO FOR IT! Call the local schools and ask when you can come in and introduce yourself to the model booker. Bring good quality photos of yourself. Buy a timer and a robe. If you've never taken a yoga class, get into one. It will help you be strong and also focused, both of which you need to be a figurative model. And if you really want to work a lot, don't complain about how hard it is. Make it look easy, even if you think you are going to die of pain. We are paid to make the hardest thing look easy. You are the muse. Inspire!

Thank you so much, Parker, for sharing your great insights and experiences.

Chapter 17

Photography

Modeling for the camera is a different experience than modeling for drawings. Key differences are:

- With photos there is no mistaking your likeness. With drawings this is often not the case, particularly with quick sketches. Although some skilled artists do produce drawings with near photo-realism, most models are more self-conscious about being recognized in nude photos than in nude drawings.

- Photography is fast. Drawings can take 20 minutes or longer per pose. Photography takes seconds. This enables a greater variety of poses, including poses that would be impossible to hold for 20 minutes. It also means the model will be changing poses frequently.

I'm going to make a distinction between two types of artistic photography modeling: reference photos and fine art photography.

Reference photos

The point of a reference photograph is to give an artist a clear view of the figure in a pose. Artists use these references when it is impractical to hire a live model. As such, reference photos are utilitarian in purpose, with little concern for composition and background imagery.

There are a few reasons why reference photos might be used:

- Sculptors work on a piece for weeks or months at a time, and they may not have the model present during the entire process.
- An artist may want to paint a very strenuous pose that is impossible to hold for more than a minute or so.
- An artist in a rural area may not have access to live models, and therefore relies on reference photos instead.

"Good lighting is the key to shooting good reference photos," advises model Ben Miller. "Have a strong light source from one direction, and another light to fill in the other side. Poorly lit photos will be grainy and show less detail."

A reference photo and a resulting drawing are shown below.

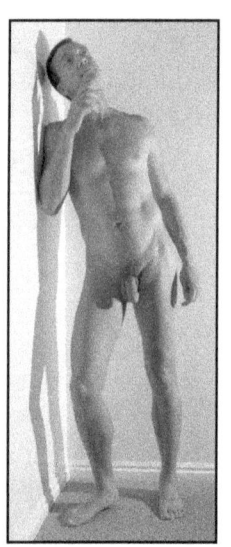 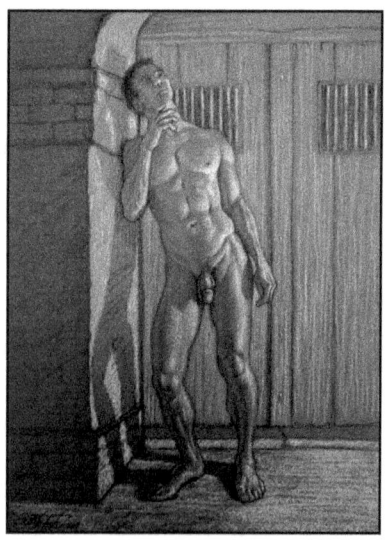

Left: © 2006 Ben Miller. Example of reference photo.
Right: © 2009 Rita Foster. Charcoal on dark gray paper.

Fine art nude photography

With fine art photography, the photograph is the finished artwork. Three common categories include:

- Studio nudes. In this category the emphasis is often on creative lighting. These are often black and white, with low-key lighting to accent the curves and angles of the body. One genre in this category is called bodyscapes, which can be thought of as using the body as a landscape, zooming in on the hills and valleys of the human form.

- Nudes in nature. The emphasis could either be on the nude or nature. In the latter case, think of Ansel Adams nature photography with one or more strategically placed nude figures. This genre can show humans in harmony with nature, and indeed part of nature.

- Body painting. This art form is not photography itself, but since it is temporary, it is usually done in conjunction with a photo shoot. Sometimes it is also done in conjunction with performance art. Body paint can be applied with a brush or sprayed on with an airbrush. Models may be required to shave body hair, and may also be required to wear a thong, particularly if the painted model will appear at a public venue. For examples of highly creative body painting, see the work of Filippo Ioco at www. iocobodyart.com

Sometimes the best shots are serendipitous. One time I was shooting with a photographer who used her garage as studio space. Afterwards, we decided to shoot some outdoor shots in her back yard. While I was waiting for her to set up, I sat in an invitingly sunny spot on the grass. When she returned from the studio with her camera she said, "Don't move! That light is perfect." We shot some variations of a few sitting and reclining

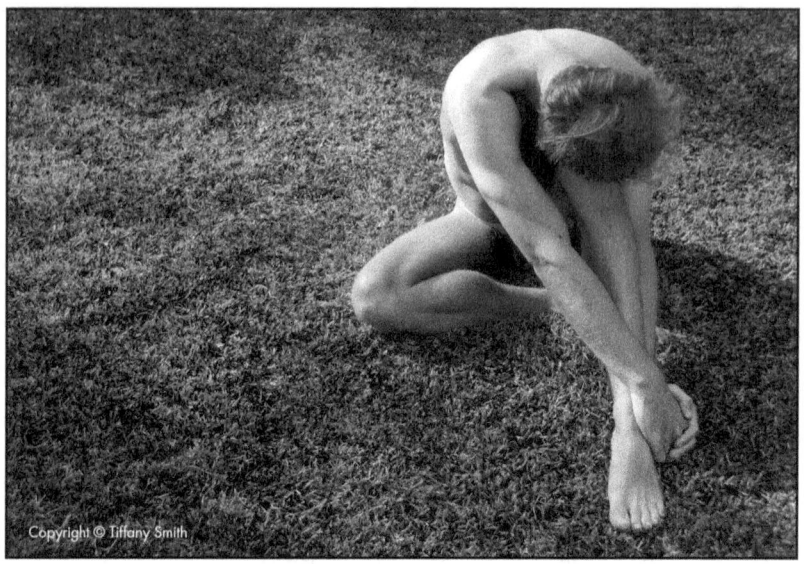

Copyright © Tiffany Smith

"Contemplation" © 2007 Tiffany Smith

poses in that spot. One of the shots turned out to be our mutual favorite. I enjoy the spontaneity of situations like this. And as I've mentioned about working with traditional artists, I enjoy the creative collaboration.

Here are some tips in preparation for a successful fine art photo shoot. In fact, these are good rules of thumb for drawing and painting sessions as well:

- Get rid of tan lines before the date of your shoot.
- Get a good night's sleep. You will not only feel better, you will look better if you are well rested and energetic during your shoot.
- For at least two hours prior to a nude photo shoot, it is advisable not to wear any clothing with elastic bands. Underwear waistbands can leave an indentation in the skin, which can take over an hour to fade. Such lines would be distracting in a photograph.

Due diligence

I am much more selective about modeling for photography than I am about modeling for the traditional arts. There is a spectrum ranging from fine art nudes to erotica to porn. My interests lie on the far end of the fine art side, but the definitions are subjective. So you need to do your own due diligence. As a first step, a look at a photographer's portfolio will give you an idea of the style, taste, and technical quality. Decide for yourself if this body of work is something you want to be a part of. The work generally speaks for itself: elegant, cheesy, creative, bland, etc.

If the photographer has no portfolio, you are probably not dealing with a professional or even a serious hobbyist. As digital SLR cameras come down in price, there are many people with equipment calling themselves photographers. The frequently asked questions page of Model Mayhem defines a term for amateur photographers with ulterior motives:

> The term GWC is an acronym for "Guy With Camera." It usually implies that said guy is only interested in photography in order to get hot ladies to get nekkid for him.[17.1]

Some female models prefer to bring an escort to a photo shoot. Some photographers will allow this, while others find this too much of a distraction. Ask the photographer for references if that makes you more comfortable.

If you don't trust the photographer, or if you are unsure about the situation, there is no point in doing the shoot. If you are nervous and hesitant, you will not make good art. Art modeling is about being free and expressive, and willing to experiment.

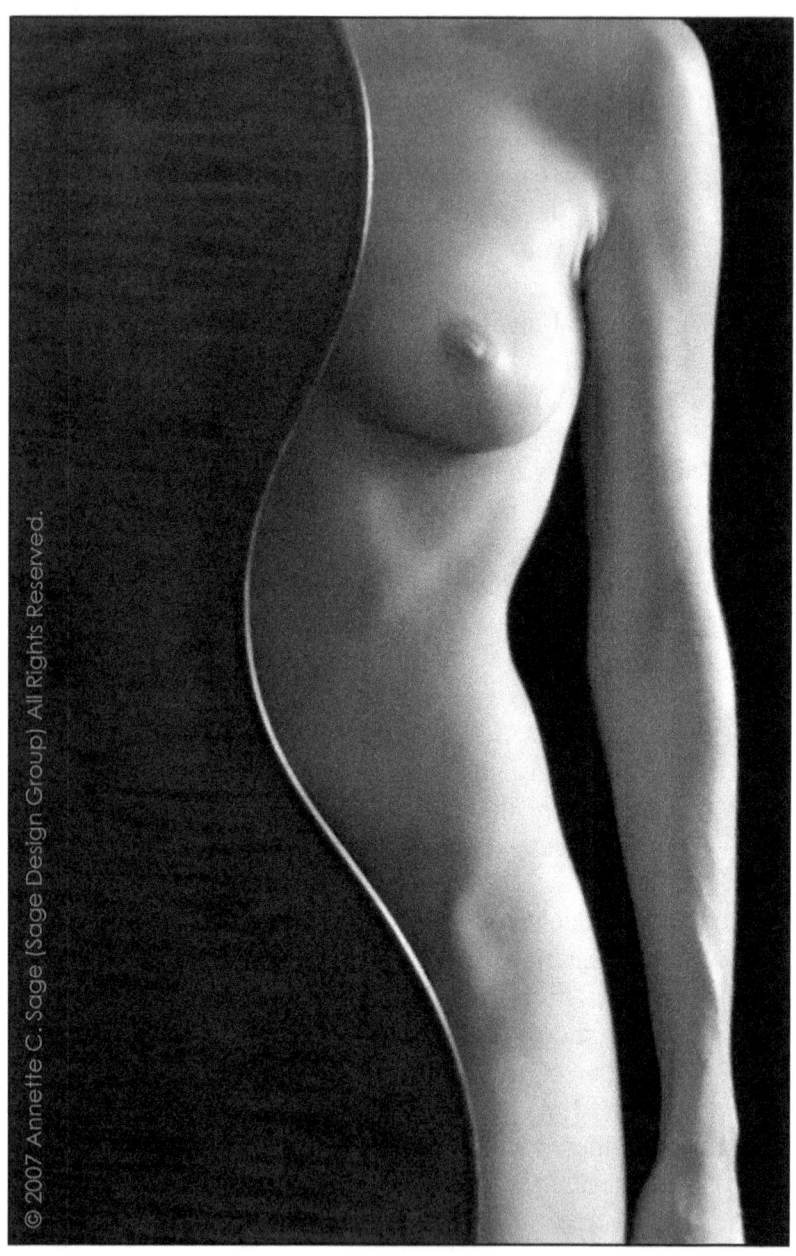

"Woman and Cello" © 2007 Annette C. Sage.

Model releases

An important thing to understand about photo shoots is the model release. Photographers automatically own the exclusive rights to the photographs they take. However, they can't publish photos of a model without a signed release from the model.

A model release is essentially a contract. A generic release may give the photographer unlimited, irrevocable rights to sell images of your likeness in any media, forever, without any further compensation. Other releases are limited in their scope. Read it carefully and understand what you are agreeing to before you sign it. Any negotiated modifications should be in writing.

Note that even without a release, the photographer owns all the rights to the photos. The model does not have any copyright or usage rights unless specifically transferred by the photographer.

A sample model release can be found in Appendix A.

Section 2257

The photographer will probably require a government-issued identification card to prove the model is at least 18 years old. The photographer must make a copy of the ID and record the model's legal name and any aliases, in order to comply with record keeping requirements under U.S. federal law, specifically 18 U.S.C. § 2257.

Section 2257 originally applied only to depictions of sexually explicit conduct. However, for works originally produced after March 18, 2009, the scope of the law was broadened, and Department of Justice interpretation is vague and subjective. The Obscenity Prosecution Task Force's 2257 Compliance Guide states:

The regulation does not define the term "lascivious exhibition of the genitals or pubic area," but the Department of Justice will rely on precedent from child pornography prosecutions for 18 U.S.C. § 2257 investigations and prosecutions involving such depictions. In that context, judicial precedent indicates that a depiction can constitute lascivious exhibition if, among other things:

(1) the focal point is on the subject's genitalia or pubic area;
(2) the setting of the visual depiction is sexually suggestive, i.e., in a place or pose generally associated with sexual activity;
(3) the visual depiction suggests sexual coyness or a willingness to engage in sexual activity; or
(4) the visual depiction is intended or designed to elicit a sexual response in the viewer.[17.2]

TFP

TFP is short for Time for Prints. This term comes from the film era of photography. In the digital age, the term TFCD is sometimes used, referring to a CD-ROM rather than prints. In this arrangement, the model receives photos rather than money for modeling services, typically done to build a portfolio.

The terms of the TFP arrangement could include actual prints, or web-quality JPEG files for an online portfolio. Often the photographer will only agree to provide a few of the "best" shots from the shoot. There could be hundreds of shots taken during a photo shoot, but most will not be used—regardless of whether it is a TFP or paid shoot—either because the pose or the photographic quality did not make the cut.

Some photographers allow the model to select their favorite shots from a contact sheet, tiny images of the whole shoot. Other photographers select the best shots themselves.

Many photographers will spend some time retouching the photos in Photoshop, or in the darkroom for a film shoot. This can be time consuming, and is another reason why only the best images are used.

Remember, the copyright is owned by the photographer, not the model. Possession of digital images does not give the model rights to alter the images or sell them.

The TFP concept can also be used with traditional artists, in which case the model receives a drawing or a print of a painting in exchange for modeling services.

Photo manipulations

One thing to keep in mind when booking photo shoots is the ubiquity of photo editing software, such as Photoshop. Some photographers simply use this as a tool to fine-tune their work, as one would do in the darkroom with film. However, others consider it an art form to combine and distort images to completely change the context of the original shoot. For example, a pose shot in the studio might be placed in a photo of a tropical island. Or a human figure might be transformed into a fantasy creature like a unicorn. But you might also find your likeness in a scene for which you would not have agreed to pose.

More jargon

There are a couple of other terms worthy of mention:

- The term "implied nude" is widely used online, on sites such as Model Mayhem. This refers to photos in which the model appears to be nude, but the genitals and female areola (nipple area) are not shown. These private parts may be covered by the model's hands, blocked from view by an object, or obscured by the camera angle. The model may or may not be completely nude during the shoot.

- Another word often used is "edgy." This can mean cutting edge or pushing the conventional boundaries, but it is ambiguous and overused to the point of becoming meaningless. If a photographer describes his shoot concept as edgy, ask for clarification.

Posing for fine art photography

Antoine de Villiers is a figurative artist whose works include drawings and paintings as well as fine art photography. Her photography has been featured in Carrie Leigh's Nude Magazine, her artwork is sold in galleries on three continents, and one of her paintings is featured on the cover of this book.

The nude figure is a prominent subject in her body of work, so she has a lot of experience working with art models. I asked Antoine to share her thoughts on modeling for a fine art nude photo shoot. Here is what she says:

I believe there is a big difference between fine art photography and any other industry like glamour or fashion. Live drawing models usually make good fine art photography models. However fashion models are trained to pose and act in a manner that will sell their attire—skills usually uncalled for in fine art work.

In my personal work, I really try to get away from the sexuality of the nude figure. I try to focus on the beauty of line and shape. I want to celebrate the figure for what it is, including its raw beauty, grace or life itself. Therefore I find it hard to work with a model wanting to look "sexy" above anything else.

I believe a good nude fine art photography model is a person passionate about art photography as well as someone truly comfortable with their figure and who they are. One can usually spot an experienced model a mile away. Experienced models know how to create shapes that work for their figure. They also do not need as much guidance and are not afraid to experiment. Being able to work well with concepts, ideas or a certain mood we aim to portray in a certain shoot is just as important as a good figure.

I would often set up a pose and ask the model to evolve the pose. For instance, in a reclining pose there are an endless number of variations for positions for your arms and legs. Sometimes subtle changes can make a huge difference in the final product. I would like every shot I take to be a little different. For example, during a three-hour shoot I normally take about 600 shots. This definitely does not consist of 600 totally different poses, but of variations of a small number of different poses. Therefore creativity is a fantastic asset for any model. I seldom get good results from a model waiting for me to set up every single pose and every variation thereof. Usually I do give a lot of guidance and regularly make suggestions, however I feel a nude art shoot is absolutely a team effort.

I think it is also crucial that a model must love the work they do. To help create the right energy I will often stop and show the model the results on my camera. Should they like what we are creating this may energize them, or at least help them to understand what direction we are heading with the shoot.

Communication is another important concept both for photographers and models. I like to set 15 minutes aside before the shoot to discuss the concept and ideas. I also try to find common ground to ensure we both get results we like. During the shoot it is important to me that the model communicates if a pose is hard to hold, if they are in pain, getting cold or even just need a break. I also enjoy hearing their ideas, should they get any during the course of the shoot.

Fine art nude photography is a different experience than traditional figurative art, but the objective is the same: to create art. So, in that respect, the collaboration between artist and art model is not so different, whether in the drawing studio or on a photo shoot.

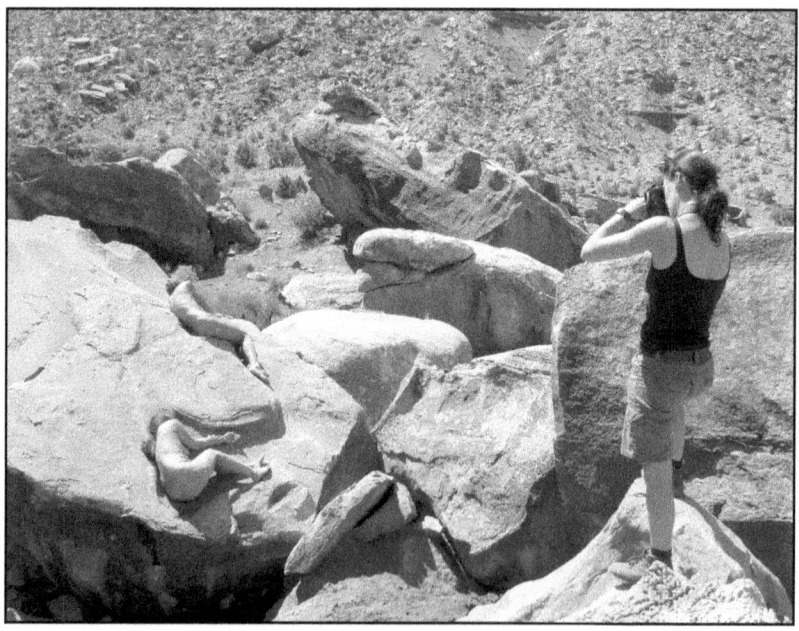

Antoine de Villiers photographs Ben and Callie on a location shoot.
© 2008 Kenneth Jaines.

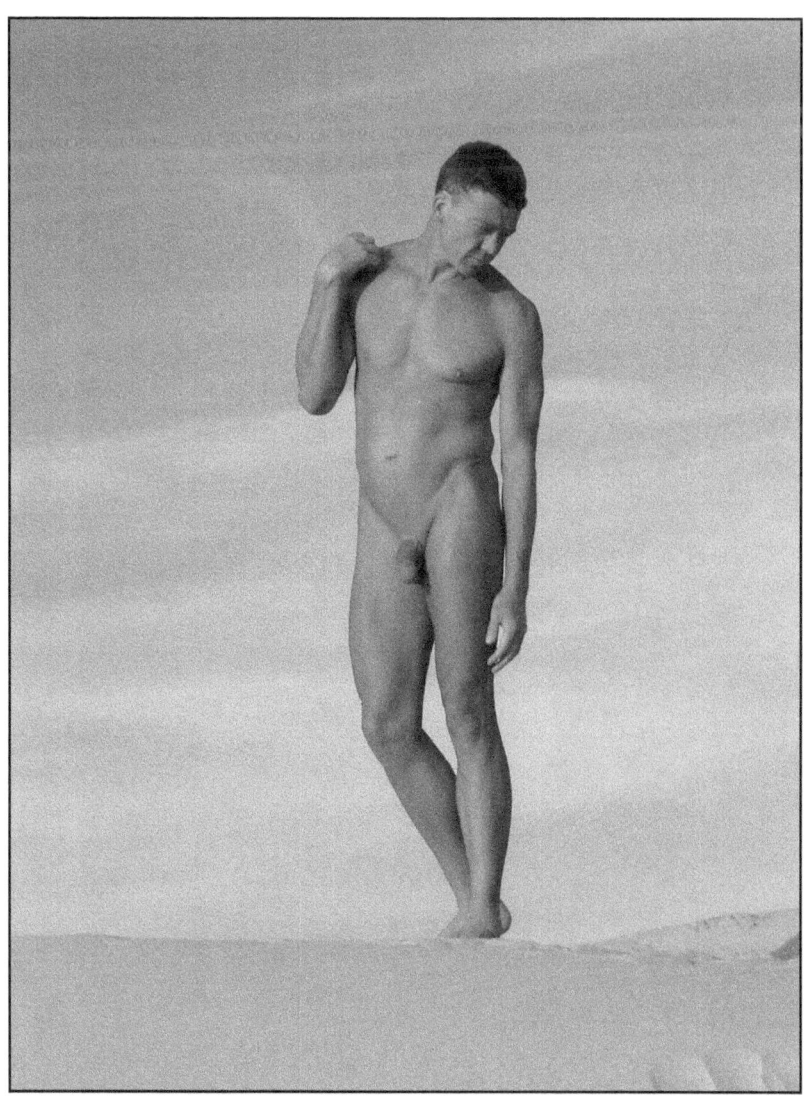

"David" © 2008 Sophronia Smith. Model: Ben Miller. Example of a contrapposto pose: notice that the weight balances on one leg, the pelvis tilts up, and the shoulders naturally tilt down to counter-balance.

Chapter 18

Interview with a Photographer: Phil Condit

Phil Condit is a multiple award-winning filmmaker, photographer and artist based in Los Angeles. His artistic work includes fine art nude photography, and he teaches workshops on the topic.

Think of the best fine art model you have worked with. What qualities made him or her such a great model?

The best models are ones comfortable in their own skin without trying to prove anything—that they are willing or daring or bold—and have a great amount of experience modeling.

The best models can offer their own interpretation to the work when you want it. A difficult model I worked with insisted on interpreting everything rather than giving me what I wanted first.

Do you direct your models on the poses you want, or do you expect models to choose poses on their own?

I usually have an idea in mind, but it is great when the model also has many of their own poses. I worked with one model whose poses were so much better than what I was thinking of that I just let her do her own thing. She was very familiar with her body and how best to present it.

Unlike fashion models, art models for traditional art come in all shapes in sizes. Is this true in fine art photography as well?

I like to work with all types of physiques when I am not pursuing a particular body type. It is hard to be too slender or too Rubenesque for me. There are a lot of photographers who work with a particular body type almost exclusively. I know one who is famous for his hard-bodied women. He prefers them muscular.

You have written, "I shoot stock for Getty Images, nature for my soul, and people and models to express my creativity." Can you talk about the creative process, and what you try to express through your images?

I am tough to pin down. I like to shoot it all. I like figure studies in which I produce studies of how light and shadow accentuate the form, transcending the body to become a graphic image. I like shooting the nude in nature as an ode to how simple things can be and how our species started out. There is an innocence to it that I love. I have a series in which I use nude and semi-nude female models to depict the roles women assume or are forced into by cultural pressure. And sometimes, I like to be outrageous. I shot two models dressed as topless ballerinas, painted white and made up to look like dolls. I had them pose as dancers and marionettes. This session expressed fun while also making a comment on how the female of our species is controlled by external forces.

You teach workshops on fine art nude photography. Tell me about that.

There are a great number of photographers who are interested in doing figure work, or nudes, who don't have a clue how to proceed. I teach the basics of not only photography but how to work with the model. I stress for the uninformed that nude photography is not about sex. The images can be sexual, but the photographer-model relationship is a business relationship. During the workshops I have the models talk to the class about nude modeling from their point of view. What they look for and what scares them away. Unfortunately, there are people who use the excuse of a camera for ulterior motives. These are the model's worst nightmare. What puts them at ease is a professional proposal which includes the location and duration of the session, what kind of work you are interested in, and a negotiated pay rate—even if it's only for prints. Be clear about how many prints. There is one thing the models and I emphasize: *do not touch the model*. This breaks the professional relationship and veers the session off track. Once a model gets nervous, you might as well pack up for the day. You won't get anything good and you'll just prolong the discomfort.

Tell me about a studio shoot.

I always have several concepts in mind when I book a model, including figure study, another couple of concepts for my "women's issues" series, and maybe some fashion. I am not much of a cheesecake photographer, so I usually don't go there. You are probably most interested in a figure study shoot, so I will just elaborate on that.

I am usually inspired by photographs of the model on their website or a site like One Model Place. I work up a concept of what I want to shoot, such as:

- White background, black background, or colored background;
- Whether I want to use any props or material;
- If I want to experiment with a different style of lighting, such as rim light, silhouetting, softbox, etc.

I book a model for half a day, four hours, unless I have a lot of work I want to accomplish; then I will go for eight. Any more than that and both the model and I get too tired to create good work. I usually hire my models because I want to work with professionals. I will work with an amateur to teach them more about modeling and to advance their career, but the work we produce is not at the same level.

Tell me about a location shoot.

A location can be an inspiration for a shoot with a model. I knew I was going to Las Vegas in the summer one year, so I booked a model to shoot at the Valley of Fire State Park, an hour outside of town. Since it was summer, I knew not too many people would be at the park and most of the campgrounds would be closed. I did most of my shooting around one of the campgrounds, out of sight of the road. It was blazing hot, over 110 degrees, but luckily the model was dressed for it.

Finding a suitable model in Las Vegas was surprisingly difficult. There are thousands of Barbie look-a-likes, but I wanted a natural looking model. When I finally found one, the negotiations began. Since we were going to a remote location, and she didn't know me, I put her at ease by hiring a friend of hers to come along as my assistant. We agreed on a price and were all set.

Another time, I was in 29 Palms outside of Joshua Tree National Park with a group of photographers and models at a Community Zoe gathering. Each photographer would hire their own model and go off shooting. We didn't do any "turkey shoots" where all the photographers shoot the same model at once, so the quality of work we produced was much better. I took one model into the Park (avoid the Rangers, they will make your life miserable) and after shooting for several hours, I broke a little early so we could stop and shoot at an abandoned house I had spotted. We did some great interiors as well as strobe shots at dusk there.

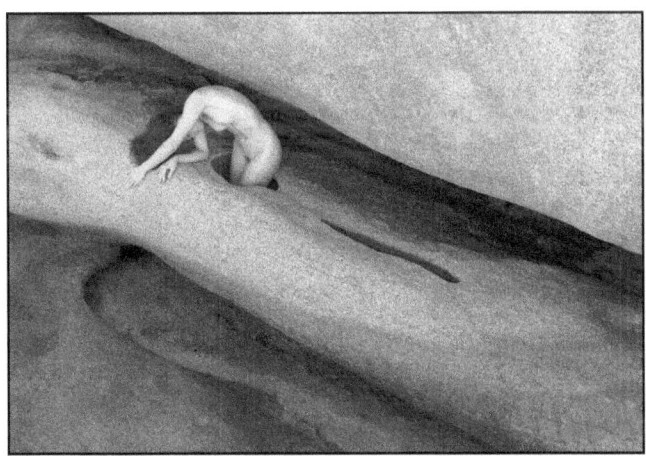

"Birth" © 2007 Philip H. Condit II. Model: Candace Nirvana.

How do you find your models?

Community Zoe, communityzoe.com, is an international group of figure photographers and models where each post their work and contact information. Models and photographers let each other know when they will be going to the other's area so they can set up shoots. All the models I have worked with from that site are professional and excellent models. Onemodelplace. com is another site to find models. They have a mixture of professional and amateur models. If you are just starting out and don't have a lot of money, you can often find an amateur model who will work for prints and experience. With the Internet, you can find whatever you want online. Post an ad on Craigslist.org and you should get several, if not many, responses.

When I first started to shoot nudes, I didn't realize that as many people wanted to be photographed in the nude as there were photographers who wanted to shoot them. There is a balance.

What advice would you give to a new model interested in a fine art nude shoot?

Be safe. If you don't know the photographer, take a friend with you. I always let models bring whomever they like; they just can't be in the studio with us. They can be within earshot, but I don't want them influencing the model's performance. One exception was a model whose boyfriend was an artist. I let him sit off to the side and sketch.

From a practical point of view, wear loose-fitting clothes that are easy on and easy off. Don't wear anything that will leave marks on your skin, such as bras and underpants. If you are modeling nude do everybody a favor and avoid tan lines. Either tan in the buff or stay out of the sun.

Chapter 19

Online Resources

Note: Online resources to find modeling jobs can be found in Chapter 11, Finding Work.

Web sources for learning more about figure modeling.

figuredrawings.com
A compilation of links about figure drawing.

cambridgelifedrawing.co.uk
A figure drawing group in England.

www.dfwartmodels.com
DFW Art Models serves the Dallas / Fort Worth, Texas area art community.

groups.yahoo.com/group/Artists-Models
Moderated by David R. Quammen, founder of the Figure Models Guild of Washington D.C. Search Yahoo Groups for other art groups in your area.

figuremodelsguild.org
Figure Models Guild of Washington D.C.

www.bayareamodelsguild.org
The Bay Area Models Guild, serving San Francisco Bay Area.

www.modelreg.co.uk
United Kingdom-based Register of Artists' Models (RAM).

www.borsheimarts.com/modeling.htm
"How to Become An Artist's Model" by Kelly Borsheim, Borsheim Art Studio.

www.posespace.com
Reference photos of figure drawing models in various poses, by the publisher of the book Art Models: Life Nudes for Drawing Painting and Sculpting by Maureen Johnson and Douglas Johnson.

human-anatomy-for-artist.com
Reference photos of figure drawing models in various poses.

www.thegreatnude.tv
A web-video magazine called The Great Nude: A Celebration of the Figurative Arts.

www.google.com
There may be other online information relevant to your area. Use search terms like "figure drawing" OR "life drawing" plus the name of your city or region. As the nature of the Web is constant change, you may discover new resources by searching from time to time.

Photo hosting

imageevent.com
If you wish to make reference photos available to selected artists, this is an excellent site. Security options include password-protected albums and hidden URLs. Accounts start at $25 per year (as of this writing in March 2009) with a free 21-day trial period.

Fine art nude photography

www.communityzoe.com

"Community Zoe is an international community of fine art nude photographers and models that make their work available to you for your viewing pleasure, for purchase, and we also offer a thriving discussion and critique area inside our discussion forum. This site is for professionals, amateurs and collectors of fine art nude photography. Many of the photographers and models who post on a regular basis can be found in photography books and magazines published internationally."

Commercial, fashion, and glamour photography

www.newmodels.com

Calling itself Modeling 101, this informative web site features over 20 articles. "The contributors to this site collectively have decades of experience in the industry in major market cities as well as secondary markets in the US, Europe and Asia, and both fashion and commercial markets."

www.zerotopia.com/resources/models/index.html

Zero Dean is a San Diego based photographer. The Advice for Models section of his web site is a great resource. Regarding portfolios Zero says, "Throw out the trash. Be selective of what you find worthy of putting on display. One good photo is more effective than 10 crappy ones. Your portfolio (printed or web version) is not a scrapbook. It is not a place to put photos simply because you want to record the fact that you had a shoot with some photographer somewhere."

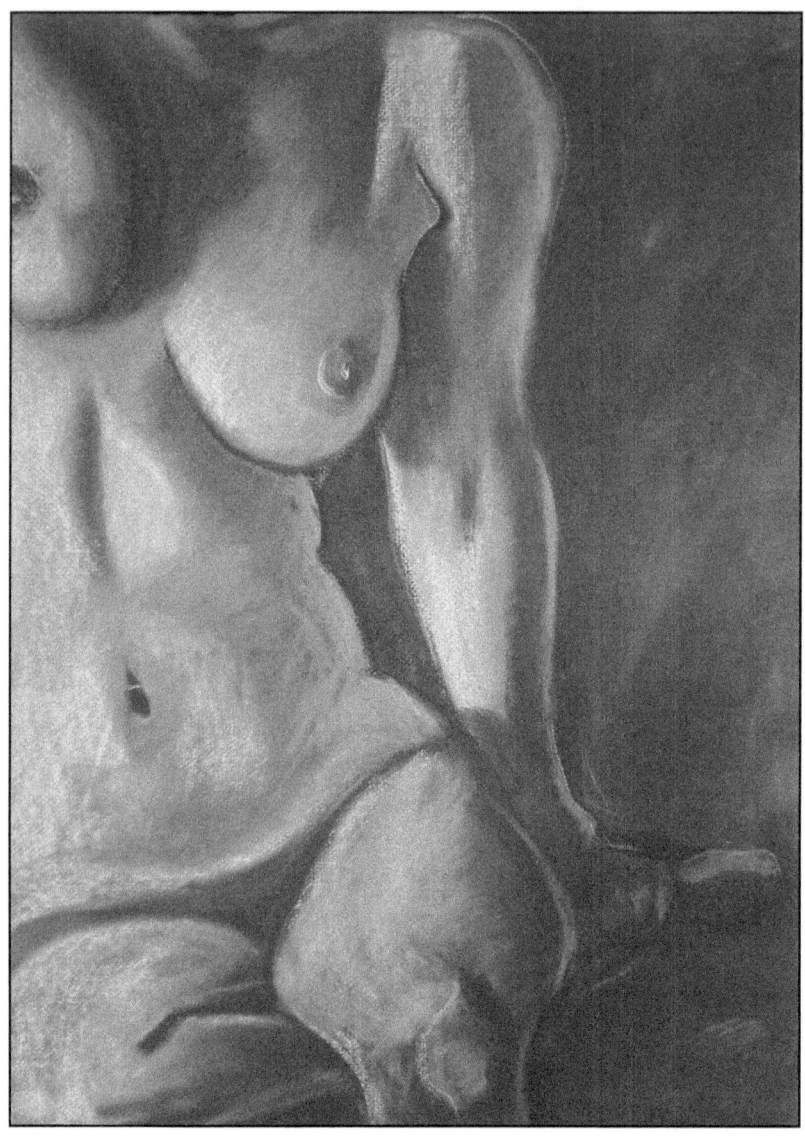

© 2005 Douglas Pexa. Example of chiaroscuro.
Charcoal, white conte, pastel on colored paper.

Chapter 20

Glossary

It is helpful to understand some of the vocabulary used by artists. Some terms refer directly to the type of pose desired. Others are words you might hear an instructor use when lecturing or advising a student. Understanding the language can help you support their objectives.

If you encounter art terms that are not included in this glossary, refer to the online art dictionary at www.artlex.com.

Asymmetry
Not the same on either side. Asymmetry generally makes a pose more interesting.

Chiaroscuro
An Italian word referring to light and dark. As an art term, refers to high contrast lighting. See drawing on page 114.

Contrapposto
Contrapposto means "counter position" in Italian. Stand with your weight shifted to one leg, causing the pelvis to tilt one side lower than the other. The shoulders will naturally tilt the opposite way to counter-balance. A prime example is Michelangelo's statue of David. See photo, page 103.

Costume drawing
Drawing of a figure wearing a special wardrobe.

Dais
The platform a model sits or stands on when modeling. Also called a model stand.

Draped figure
Model wearing clothes.

Drawing from life
Drawing from a live model.

Figure
The human body.

Figure drawing
Drawing the human body. Usually refers to drawing nude figures.

Foreshortening
Objects close to us appear bigger than objects far away. A foreshortened pose is one in which one part of the body is closer to the artist than the rest. If the model points her finger toward the artists with her arm fully extended, the arm would be foreshortened; the hand would be drawn disproportionately large, and the shoulder would appear disproportionately small. In a reclining pose, the entire body can be foreshortened. See drawing on page 32.

Gesture Drawing
Can be a quick warm-up drawing that looks like a stick figure, except generally more loose and curvy. Can also be a first step to capture the overall pose, before building up a more detailed drawing. See examples of page 45.

Gesture Pose
Short, dynamic poses often done in quick succession at the beginning of a figure drawing class.

Life drawing
Drawing the nude human body.

Model Stand
The platform a model sits or stands on when modeling. Also called a dais.

Musculature
The anatomy of the muscular system.

Muse
Source of inspiration. A model can be an artist's muse.

Negative space
A model may be asked to choose a pose with interesting negative space. Think of the figure as positive space, and any open areas as negative spaces. For example, when you put your hand on your hip with the elbow pointing out, the triangular shape between the arm and the torso is called a negative space. A fetal position has very little negative space. See painting on page 33.

Perspective
In a classroom, the model stand may be in the middle of the room with students positioned on all sides. They're all drawing the same pose, but from a different perspective. Artists are trained to draw "what they see, not what they know." Even though your brain knows a foot has five toes, from a certain angle you may only be able to see two.

Proportion
One of the fundamental challenges of a beginning artist is drawing the body parts in proper proportion. The height of the human body is roughly the size of eight heads.

Reference photo
A photograph of a pose used by an artist to draw, paint, or sculpt while the live model is not present.

Shadows
There are two types of shadows. A cast shadow is caused by an object blocking the light source, such as the shadow of a person on the sidewalk. A form shadow is on the dark side of an object, facing away from the light source. Cast shadows have hard edges whereas form shadows have soft edges. This is something to be aware of in the context of creating interesting lighting. Many art classrooms have a spotlight in order to create more dramatic shadows on the model.

Simplified form
Drawing the body by representing its components as spheres, cones, and cubes.

Tone
Refers to shading.

Undraped
Synonym for Nude.

Values
The value is the degree of light or shadow. The range of values is the spectrum from the lightest light to the darkest dark.

Appendix A

Sample Model Release

Courtesy of Antoine de Villiers

In consideration of my engagement as a model, upon the terms herewith stated, I hereby give to (Photographer's Name), his/her heirs, legal representatives and assigns, those for whom (Photographer's Name) is acting, and those acting with his/her authority and permission:

a) the unrestricted right and permission to copyright and use, re-use, publish, and republish photographic portraits or pictures of me or in which I may be included intact or in part, composite or distorted in character or form, without restriction as to changes or transformations in conjunction with a fictitious name, or reproduction hereof in color or otherwise, made through any and all media now or hereafter known for illustration, art, promotion, advertising, trade, or any other purpose whatsoever.

b) I also permit the use of any printed material in connection therewith.

c) I hereby relinquish any right that I may have to examine or approve the completed product or products or the advertising copy or printed matter that may be used in conjunction therewith or the use to which it may be applied.

d) I hereby release, discharge and agree to save harmless (Photographer's Name), his/her heirs, legal representatives or assigns, and all persons functioning under her permission or authority, or those for whom she is functioning, from any liability by virtue of any blurring, distortion, alteration, optical illusion, or use in composite form whether intentional or otherwise, that may occur or be produced in the taking of said pictures or in any subsequent processing thereof, as well as any publication thereof, including without limitation any claims for libel or invasion of privacy.

e) I hereby affirm that I am over the age of 18 and have the right to contract in my own name. I have read the above authorization, release and agreement, prior to its execution; I fully understand the contents thereof. This agreement shall be binding upon me and my heirs, legal representatives and assigns.

Modeling Fee: $_____
OR
TFP terms: _____

Dated: _____

Signed: _____

Print Name: _____

Address: _____

City: _____

State/Zip: _____

Appendix B

Model's Protocol

by Nancy Lilly

As a model, you are expected to:

1. Be at the booking, on the model stand, and ready to work at the time agreed upon.
2. Time your poses and breaks accurately.
3. Create your poses based on the stated needs of teacher, class, workshop, or artist.
4. Hold your poses like a rock. And if it hurts, don't let your face show the pain.
5. Do not talk on the model stand unless you are explicitly asked a question.

Models deal with a major paradox:

- The model is the **most important** person in the studio.
- The model has the **least power** of anyone in the studio.

If you are not there, the teacher cannot teach, and the students cannot draw, paint, or sculpt. Even if the instructor is planning to lecture, he/she is nervous as a cat, not knowing if or when you will arrive. You are the necessary center of attention, the inspiration, and the learning tool for whatever will transpire in the class, workshop, or artist's studio. Without you, the painting, drawing, sculpture will not exist! It all falls apart without your presence. If you are not there, the people waiting for you get frustrated, confused, disappointed, and finally angry.

That's how important you are.

Your job is to be there on the model stand and ready to work at the time agreed upon. Be sure your cell phone is turned off. It's OK if the teacher is late. It's OK if a student is late. It is <u>not OK</u> for the model to be late. Be sure you understand the project (lesson, point of view) of the class, workshop, or artist. And then hold your pose like a rock no matter how stressful, uncomfortable, or painful it may be. Keep your mouth shut when you are on the model stand unless your input is requested. Hold your pose for the required time and don't stretch your breaks. If there's a lecture or a critique, stay and listen to it—you will learn more about what is needed for the session. You are there to do what they need. Do not offer your opinion about anything unless you are asked.

That's how little power you have.

CANCELING: When you are booked for something, it is very often because you are the very special person with the specific attributes and abilities needed. That is why canceling the booking can create a major problem for the group or teacher. Yes, cancellations can be unavoidable. That is understood. But if you cancel at the last minute because of a "better" booking, and assume that it's OK because you found another model to fill the time slot, you can really mess things up for the group. Frequently, they specifically need your height, your coloring, your structure, your abilities, your special costume, your personality, etc. When you send another model it can blow their project all to hell!

If you are an actor or dancer or musician, it is unfair to take bookings and assume that canceling for an audition is appropriate. It isn't. You have made a creative and a business commitment. People are depending upon you to honor it.

Again, you are an individual so you are not easily replaceable. That's your strength, but because it is your special quality it is also your weakness. It's why you also are not booked for some jobs that just don't fit. In some situations, what is needed is a good, reliable, functioning model. Period. But frequently your special qualities are needed to motivate the creative process. You can't be replaced. You can only be "substituted for."

If canceling is unavoidable and you do try to find a "replacement" model, check with the artist or the person doing the booking before you take the responsibility of sending the new model. Often it will work out, but often it won't. Better to get it straight ahead of time. It is possible that the class project is based on a thin, black, male, gesture model. So if you send a heavy, pale, static, female model as a replacement, it sure isn't going to work!

TALKING: When the model takes a pose, he/she creates a gesture, mood, form, story, and inspiration for the artists, who become immersed in the model's creation. When a model then opens his/her mouth and starts talking, the artist's concentration and the entire mood the model worked to create are destroyed. The model who talks from the model stand is his/her own worst enemy.

"Well, I would really love to use so-and-so, but he/she talks from the model stand so please don't schedule that person for my class anymore." Believe me, I've heard that many a time!

You enjoy your work much more when there is a creative synergy with the artist or class with whom you are working. As a professional you deserve respect and appreciation for your professionalism. Occasionally, the situation can be one that is uncomfortable, unprofessional, and unfulfilling in many ways. Of course, you will complete the booking with professionalism—barring a situation that is untenable—but your strength is that you have the option to not work that particular venue anymore.

Appendix C

Memo to Art Models

This is a sample memorandum from the model booker to new models. Based on a document provided courtesy of Nancy Lilly, retired model manager for Art Center College of Design and Chouinard Foundation.

All models must have a Model Application and Agreement filled out and signed and must have one or more photos on file. When you arrive for your first booking, you will fill out a brief form with your pay information that will be filed with the business office so they can issue your check. If your annual earnings at XYZ College exceed $600, you will be issued a 1099 form for income tax purposes.

Allow yourself enough time to sign in and change clothes. **You are expected to be on the model stand and ready to work at the time for which you have been scheduled.** If you are going to be late, you must call to notify us and let us know when to expect you. If you fail to call before class time, a substitute model will be hired and your pay will be forfeited.

Extra pay allotments may be made for costumes, props, drapery, etc. at my discretion using guidelines set down by the business office. Please confer with me if you have any questions on this.

If it becomes necessary for you to cancel a booking, please let me know as soon as possible so I can schedule a replacement. **Do not send a replacement model to fill in without clearing it with me first**. If an emergency arises, you may contact me at home.

It is against XYZ College policy to cancel models when a booking has been confirmed. Occasionally an exception must be made due to unforeseen circumstances. If it becomes necessary for me to cancel your booking, I will do my best to give you a replacement booking as soon as possible, or if the cancellation is "last minute" (within one business week) and no replacement booking is available, XYZ College will pay you for the time lost.

If the teacher gives a lecture, critique, or other presentation, I recommend that you remain in the studio in order to learn the specific needs and goals of the teacher and the students. It will enable you to be a more creative and effective model. After working with an instructor long enough to be familiar with his/her procedures and point of view, you may wish to use lectures, critiques, etc., as "break" time. In that case, please remain close to the studio and aware of the progress of the class. **You are responsible for being available and ready to work as soon as you are needed. It should never be necessary for a teacher to have to look for you.**

The security of our models is very important to XYZ College. We wish to protect your privacy. Our studios will be closed to visitors and tours. If an exception is to be made, it will be only with both the teacher's and the model's permission.

Unless booked specifically for photography or film classes, you are not expected to pose for photographs, videos, etc. without your express permission. In case of any misunderstandings with staff, faculty, or students about use of cameras in a classroom situation, notify the office immediately.

Your reliability, punctuality, and professional attitude are appreciated as much as your modeling ability. They are definite factors taken into account when we are deciding on bookings and have a very real effect on how frequently you will be hired at XYZ College.

PLEASE:

- Be on time.
- Clarify modeling instructions, break times, and procedures with the teacher.
- If posing nude or semi-nude, wear an appropriate robe or cover up when not on the model stand.
- Wear appropriate footwear in the studio.
- Bring your own watch or timer so you can time your poses and your breaks accurately.
- While on the model stand, the model should be modeling or listening to the instructor.
- Turn off your cell phone and MP3 player before entering the studio. Do not use these items in the studio, even on your break.
- Refrain from unnecessary conversation while on the model stand.
- Do not smoke inside the building, and do not bring food or drinks into the studio.
- Please do not bring your pet(s) with you.

Thank you for the creativity and inspiration that you bring to XYZ College.

Appendix D

Art Model Policy for Faculty

In support of professional standards, college art departments and workshop leaders are encouraged to adopt this policy. It may be downloaded for free at www.artmodelbook.com. This policy is based on a document provided courtesy of Nancy Lilly, retired model manager for Art Center College of Design and Chouinard Foundation.

Faculty will submit Model Request Forms as soon as possible before a class is to begin. This will help to ensure scheduling of appropriate support, based upon the focus of their class(es). Last minute bookings are often difficult to arrange.

If a model's booking is canceled by the school—through no fault of the model—five business days or less before the scheduled booking, the school will pay the model unless a replacement booking can be scheduled during that business week. If the booking is canceled through fault of the model, no payment will be made.

Model pay scale will remain consistent with other schools and departments of art. Models will be paid for a minimum of three hours per session, even if a class is shorter or the model is dismissed early. Extra pay allotments may be made for costumes, draperies, special make-up, etc. at the discretion of the school.

The number of models allowed per class is based upon the number of students in the class, the type of class, the needs of the instructor, and the budget. Requests for extra models should go through the office, where the needs can be balanced with the budget. Often, even in a small class, a compositional problem necessitates the use of two (or more) models on an occasional basis.*

Due to budget, insurance, and organizational considerations, bookings <u>must</u> be done through the school, and models who are to be booked <u>must</u> have paperwork on file with XYZ College. Individual bookings by faculty will not be honored; the model will not be allowed to pose and will not be paid.

Problems with models should be dealt with privately, not in front of the class. Sometimes a model's abilities and personality fit well in one class but not in another. Give feedback to the person booking the models.

The following must be cleared ahead of time:
- Figure models working together on the same stand.
- Male and female models posing nude in same studio.

Safety considerations—safety has priority before aesthetics. No model should be expected to work in an unsafe or insecure environment. Any posing on higher than usual stands, on ladders, or other non-traditional settings must be cleared with the model at the time of the booking, not at the last minute.

Models are to receive a five-minute rest break after each 20-25 minute posing session. If a longer posing time is required for some reason, this must be cleared with the model before the pose begins. Holding a pose is more strenuous than it may appear. This recovery period is industry standard.

No unauthorized people are allowed to enter the studio when a model is posing nude. In case of visitors, tours, etc., permission from both teacher and model must be given. The model is to be given the opportunity to put on a robe and take a break while visitors go through.

No cameras are allowed in the studio. Photos, videos, etc. are prohibited unless specific permission has been given and releases have been signed.

Students may not pose nude. In the event a model does not show up, students may take turns posing, but must remain clothed. Privacy is very important for the security of the model. If a model is both attending classes and figure modeling at a school, he or she is too vulnerable.

Do not touch the model without permission. To point out lighting or anatomy features, a laser pointer is advised.

Model stands are for the use of models and for set-ups designated by faculty. They are not for student use as an easel substitute, picnic table, etc. Models should be supplied with fans or space heaters as necessary and given a clean environment in which to work.

Location projects – The model, as well as the students, must sign a location waiver. This must be done before the location trip and be on file at the time of the trip.

Models are vulnerable, particularly when they are working for a figure class. A good model is working harder and hurting more than you will ever know unless you have done it yourself. The respect and appreciation that XYZ College, its faculty, and students show toward the models will influence how much effort the models make.

*XYZ College budget guidelines for booking two models:
  - 20 or more students in a figure drawing class.
  - 18 or more students in a painting class
  - 16 or more students in any class that needs the student to be involved with detail (such as portraiture).

Appendix E

Memo to Faculty on Scheduling Models

This is a sample memorandum from the model booker to faculty, regarding scheduling procedures. This document does not apply to schools where the instructor books models directly. Courtesy of Nancy Lilly, retired model manager for Art Center College of Design and Chouinard Foundation.

If you wish to use models in your classes, the sooner you can advise me of your desired schedule, the better the chances are that I will be able to book the specific individuals or types that you require. Model request forms are available for you, and I would appreciate it if you would fill out a form each term for me to have on file. Last minute bookings are often difficult to arrange. Normal scheduling must be given priority and last minute requests will be attempted only if they do not interfere with regular duties.

If you expect to plan a session for which a model will not be needed, let me know at the beginning of the term. It is against policy to cancel a model once a booking is confirmed. If other arrangements cannot be made, XYZ College is obligated to pay the model even if he/she did not work.

The number of models who can be booked per class session is determined by the type of class, the number of students enrolled in the class, the budget, and your individual needs. Please check with me if you have questions about model usage, allocation, extra models, etc. I will do the best I can to accommodate your needs and balance them with the school's budget constraints. Do not arrange for a model on your own for a XYZ College class. Insurance, scheduling, and budget considerations make it essential that models are scheduled specifically through the school.

If you would like a particular model to work a particular class, and you have not made that request in advance, <u>please</u> discuss that with the office, <u>not</u> with the model.

I'll do my best to match the right model(s) with your classes, but please be aware that cancellations, scheduling conflicts, and other problems occur that can necessitate unavoidable substitutions on occasion.

If a model does not hold poses well, is careless about break times, or is unprofessional in any way that impacts your class, please either point out the problem to the model (privately) or let me know so that I can take care of it. If a model works well for your needs and you wish him/her to be hired again, please let me know. Tell me directly instead of asking the model to tell me so that we may avoid any possible misunderstandings.

Sometimes a model's abilities and personality fit well in one class but not in another, so it is very helpful to have feedback from you.

If you are planning to use two figure models and wish them to pose on the same stand, or if a male and a female model are to work nude or partially nude in the same studio, it is necessary for me to clear this ahead of time with the models concerned. Please let me know your plans, so we can avoid possible last minute problems.

OFF-CAMPUS

If you plan to take a model to an off-campus location, it will be necessary to have the model fill out a location waiver and file it with the office <u>before</u> the date of the class meeting. Waiver forms for both models and students will be available.

GUIDELINES

PLEASE:
- Tell your model at the beginning of class what will be required for the session. Do not expect a model to continue a pose for more than 25 minutes unless the extension of time was agreed to before the pose began.
- Clarify your break times and procedures with the model. A five-minute rest period for each 20 to 25 minutes worked is necessary.
- Be aware of the need for safety. A model should not be expected to pose in an uncomfortable, unnerving,* or potentially dangerous situation (on an unstable support, on top of a ladder, etc.). Be sure that lights and any props are stable and balanced.

PLEASE DO NOT:
- Allow cameras of any kind in the studio.
- Allow visitors or tours in the studio when a model is posing nude or semi-nude.
- Touch the model without permission.

Please give me suggestions and let me know how I can help you. Your input is necessary.

* Modeling is inherently hard and uncomfortable work, but a model should not be expected to work in a situation that is physically or emotionally excessive. If you wish something that you feel is out of the ordinary, please let it be cleared with the model when the booking is being made. Some models can take a difficult standing pose for three hours; some cannot. Some models are not afraid of heights; some are. Some models are comfortable working closely with other models; some are not. The needs of your classes are the priority, and planning ahead will enable you to have what you need.

End Notes

1.1   "Sean Connery," Wikipedia.

2.1   Marshall, 133.
2.2   Marshall, 140.
2.3   Marshall, 109.
2.4   The Naturist Society.
2.5   Register of Artists' Models.
2.6   Borsheim.
2.7   Borsheim.
2.8   Rooney, 25.

6.1   Newberry.
6.2   Rooney, 85.
6.3   "Fainting." Penn State Children's Hospital.
6.4   Hirsch.
6.5   Rubin.

7.1   Vilppu, 7.

11.1   Speedo is a brand name, but colloquially the term
        refers to men's swim briefs.
11.2   Bay Area Models Guild.
11.3   DFW Art Models.
11.4   Phillips, 115.

13.1   Rubin.

17.1   Model Mayhem.
17.2   "2257 Compliance Guide."

Bibliography

"2257 Compliance Guide." United States Department of Justice. http://www.usdoj.gov/criminal/optf/links/2257-compliance-guide.html. Accessed April 23, 2009.

Bay Area Model's Guild. www.bayareamodelsguild.org.

Borsheim, Kelly. "How to Become An Artist's Model." www.borsheimarts.com/modeling.htm.

DFW Art Models - Frequently Asked Questions. www.dfwartmodels.com/faq.php.

"Fainting." Health and Disease Information, Penn State Children's Hospital. www.hmc.psu.edu/childrens/healthinfo/f/fainting.htm. Accessed March 14, 2009.

Hirsch, Larissa, M.D., "Why Does My Foot Fall Asleep?" July 2007. KidsHealth. kidshealth.org/kid/talk/qa/foot_asleep.html. Accessed March 14, 2009.

Marshall, John R., M.D., Social Phobia: From Shyness to Stage Fright. New York: BasicBooks, 1994.

Model Mayhem. www.modelmayhem.com/faqs.php.

The Naturist Society. www.naturistsociety.com.

Newberry, Michael. "A Manifesto." June 2007. michaelnewberry.com/video/video.htm.

Phillips, Sarah R., Modeling Life: Art Models Speak about Nudity, Sexuality, and the Creative Process. Albany: State University of New York Press, 2006.

Register of Artists' Models, Consultative Guidelines. www.modelreg.co.uk/4.htm.

Rooney, Kathleen. Live Nude Girl: My Life as an Object. Fayetteville: The University of Arkansas Press, 2008.

Rubin, Michael, M.D. "Mononeuropathy." The Merck Manual of Medical Information, Second Home Edition. Revised February 2008. www.merck.com/mmhe/print/sec06/ch095/ch095f.html. Accessed March 14, 2009.

"Sean Connery," Wikipedia. en.wikipedia.org/wiki/Sean_Connery.

Vilppu, Glenn V. The Vilppu Drawing Manual. Acton, CA: Vilppu Studio Press, 1997.

Acknowledgements

I would like to thank Nancy Lilly for her invaluable contributions to this project. She generously shared stories, insights, and documents which greatly improved the book.

I am deeply grateful to Art Krummel for his expert guidance.

Thanks to André Guimond, Kenneth Jaines, Joseph Larkin, Jan Maly, Wendy McClay-Triplett, and Dee Overly for reading the manuscript at various stages and offering very helpful feedback.

Thanks to Antoine de Villiers for the cover art and her generous contribution to the photography chapter.

I would like to acknowledge the encouragement and support of Lee Penrod.

Thanks to everyone who was interviewed, for sharing their insights. Their names appear throughout this book.

Thanks also to all of the artists and photographers who gave permission to include their work in this book. Their names appear in the captions under their work.

Finally, thanks to all of the artists, photographers, art instructors, and art students who contributed to my experience as an art model. You all helped to make this book possible.

www.ingramcontent.com/pod-product-compliance
Lightning Source LLC
Chambersburg PA
CBHW051533170526
45165CB00002B/712